内蒙古城市风貌特色系列图书

鄂尔多斯城韵
CHARMING ORDOS

Urban Feature of Inner Mongolia Series Book

宫秉祥 主编

Editor-in-chief: Bingxiang Gong

中国建筑工业出版社
CHINA ARCHITECTURE & BUILDING PRESS

图书在版编目（CIP）数据

鄂尔多斯城韵 / 宫秉祥主编. —— 北京：中国建筑工业出版社，2013.12
（内蒙古城市风貌特色系列图书）
ISBN 978-7-112-16274-1

Ⅰ. ①鄂… Ⅱ. ①宫… Ⅲ. ①城市建设-研究-鄂尔多斯市 Ⅳ. ①F299.272.63

中国版本图书馆CIP数据核字(2013)第312812号

责任编辑：张振光　杜一鸣　王雁宾
装帧设计：肖晋兴
责任校对：姜小莲

内蒙古城市风貌特色系列图书
鄂尔多斯城韵
宫秉祥　主编
＊
中国建筑工业出版社出版、发行（北京西郊百万庄）
各地新华书店、建筑书店经销
北京晋兴抒和文化传播有限公司制版
北京画中画印刷有限公司印刷
＊
开本：787×1092毫米　1/16　印张：23½　字数：715千字
2014年1月第一版　2014年1月第一次印刷
定价：198.00元
ISBN 978-7-112-16274-1
　　　（25024）

版权所有　翻印必究
如有印装质量问题，可寄本社退换
（邮政编码　100037）

《鄂尔多斯城韵》编撰委员会名单

顾　　问：郝益东　李振东　张鹏举　杨永胜

主　　任：云光中　廉　素

副 主 任：宫秉祥

委　　员：陈旭辉　史贵俊　谢东平　王景山
　　　　　　王道尔吉　任光飞　王凤莲

总 编 撰：郝益东

主　　编：宫秉祥

副 主 编：王凤莲

撰　　稿：郝益东　王凤莲　刘　域　张鹏举　王　斌

图文编辑：闫慧玲　刘贵峰　田　伟　李　甜　王　斌

本册提供图片资料者名单

提供图片单位：

鄂尔多斯市规划局	鄂尔多斯市委宣传部
鄂尔多斯市文化局	鄂尔多斯市成吉思汗陵管委会
鄂尔多斯市建委园林局	康巴什新区管委会
伊金霍洛旗规划局	鄂托克旗规划局
鄂托克前旗规划局	乌审旗规划局
杭锦旗规划事业服务中心	达拉特旗规划局
准格尔旗规划局	鄂尔多斯市博远城市规划设计有限公司

提供图片个人（按姓氏笔画为序）：

王　斌　　王浩锡　　布日金　　史贵俊　　刘宏宇　　刘伟东

杜一鸣　　张鹏举　　杨立科　　杨　瑞　　郝益东　　郝常明

奥静波　　戴东辉

目录 Content

	导论 Introduction	6
	第一章　应势而城 Chapter One　City out of Complexion	23
	第二章　鄂尔多斯城市群 Chapter Two　Urban Agglomeration in Ordos	57
	第三章　中心城区形态与布局 Chapter Three　Center City Layout and Form	89
	第四章　园林广场 Chapter Four　Garden & Square	157
	第五章　建筑风貌 Chapter Five　Architectural Features	239
	第六章　雕塑与装饰 Chapter Six　Sculptures & Decoration	313

导论
Introduction

在国内外对"都市雾霾"的热议中，人们越来越怀念"白天看到蓝天，晚上见到星空"的自然环境。然而环顾周围就会发现，只有到高原城市才可能享受到清洁、自然而又现代的人居环境。其中距离首都北京500公里的鄂尔多斯市以其海拔千米之余、环境本底无污染的优势居于独特超群的地位。

一、宜居环境聚焦千米高原

在当今世界，平原城市、沿海城市、河流中下游城市遇到的一个共同顽症，就是空气、水源、土壤的污染越来越严重。特别是在人口稠密的国家，生态环境的宜居性越来越聚焦在地势较高的城市。

宜居性向高地势回归是历史趋势

在石器时代，人类为了躲避洪水和海浸，猎采到种类丰富的动植物，以及制造大量工具的方便性，高原地域便成为古人最适宜的生存栖息地。目前我国境内发现的万年以前的古人类遗址，如云南元谋、北京周口店、陕西蓝田、内蒙古大窑、扎赉诺尔、萨拉乌苏（河套人）、乌兰木伦等遗址都存在于海拔较高的地区。人类社会进入农业文明之后，平原的优势逐渐显现出来，城池和村落也大都出现在冲积平原上。而近几百年的工业文明及大航海时代，则造就了异军突起的沿海港口城市。然而，人类文明进入信息化和后工业时代后，构成城市宜居性的环境、资源、经济、社会条件均面临着重新"洗牌"，地势较高城市的资源环境优势随之凸显。20世纪后半期世界上最负盛名的两个新建城市巴西的巴西利亚和印度的昌迪加尔都坐落在海拔较高的地方。

大陆性气候阻滞"亚洲棕云"

发端于北印度洋沿岸的"亚洲棕云"在1999年被发现时，主要影响地区只限于南亚次大陆和东南亚。十几年来随着工业排放、交通废气、秸秆焚烧、林草火灾、火山喷发等诱发因素不断加剧，"亚洲棕云"的厚度已达数公里，波及范围不仅包括亚洲南部和东部的整个海洋性气候区域，而且影响到了北美西部和非洲北部。据报道连宇航员从国际空间站观察地球这一区域时也发现"蓝色少了，变模糊了"。然而，属于大陆性气候的高原地区却基本不在"亚洲棕云"的经常性漂移范围之内，而这也正是到这些地方总能体验到空气清新的基础条件。

细颗粒污染的震撼倒逼区域布局的调整

近些年来，大中城市以飘尘（直径小于10微米的颗粒污染物即PM10）为指标开展空气污染防治，大都得出优良天数逐年增加的结论。但是表面上飘尘总量的下降并未减缓污染程度的实质性增强。因为污染物的构成更加恶化了。城乡燃烧排放、机动车尾气、工业品挥发、跨区域漂移导致细颗粒物（直径小于2.5微米即PM2.5）的比例持续增加使得城市雾霾越来越严重。特别是冬春季节沿海城市和平原城市雾霾天气过程首尾相接的现实，促使人们对空气污染的恐慌从过去关注较大颗粒的"尘"转移到细颗粒的"霾"。在"人人喊打灰霾"的声浪中，对产业布局、能源结构、城市功能、环保标准进行全面调整优化势在必行。资源性产业向原料的附近转移，能源生产向清洁能源富集区转移已经提上日程。而环境容量大、自净作用强、可再生能源丰富的地区既有承担调整的责任，也有谋求发展的机遇。建设千米高原现代生态宜居城市恰逢其时。

建设宜居鄂尔多斯的自然环境优势

鄂尔多斯市处于大陆性气候控制和海洋性气候影响的交汇地带。就中心城区来讲，各种自然环境条件都具有适宜、适中、易于趋利避害的优越性。

海拔适中。1100—1400多米的海拔高度形成了气压适宜、氧气充足、有利于人体健康的环境条件。

温度适宜。年平均白日（最高）气温摄氏12度左右，冬无极寒，夏无酷暑，四季分明而舒适。

湿度较好。黄河环绕市域三面，大小支流纵横分布，中心城区年平均降水量达390毫米，月平均相对湿度一般在40%~60%之间。

光照充足。年平均日照时数达3100小时，日照率70%左右，仿佛是天然"大光吧"。

空气流动性好。中心城区处于开阔平坦的波状高原，周边无高山、沙丘阻挡。年平均风速3.5米/秒左右。沙尘暴易发的4月份平均风速4.5米/秒左右。风向以西北风为多。这些特点既有利于抵御东部沿海污染性"棕云"的侵入，又有利于维持城区空气的清新状态。

生物多样性强。市域内土质较好，平均积温可达2800℃，有利于各种植物的生长。境内分布着沙地疏林草原、典型草原、荒漠草原和沙漠湖滨草甸。林草植被建设和生态修复的条件较好。总体上空气、土壤、地下水环境本底无污染，可以就近就地生产有机、无公害的各种动物性和植物性食品。

2011年鄂尔多斯市百岁以上老人

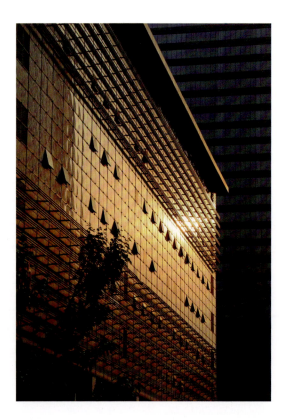

达25人,有的旗曾接近世界"长寿之乡"百岁老人达到十万分之七点五的标准。这从一个侧面反映出随着经济社会和城乡建设的协调发展,鄂尔多斯的宜居性潜能正在释放,并惠及全体居民。

二、宜居城市破解"资源诅咒"

20世纪80年代,改革开放的洪流把资源富集、区位优越的鄂尔多斯推到开发建设的前沿。正值此时,国内外出现的"资源枯竭"实例和"资源诅咒"理论也迫使人们对如何实现协调发展和可持续发展的路径进行权衡抉择。

所谓"资源诅咒",简单而言就是一窝蜂地采掘自然资源,"挤出"了其他发展要素,扼杀了长远发展机会,最终导致原料、资金、人气统统外流,资源产地却以贫困和废墟为结局。破解这一"诅咒胜者"厄运的有效途径就是构建"资源开发—产业发展—宜居城市建设"同时兼顾的崭新格局。

以"资源换资金"启动发展

鄂尔多斯地上地下资源都很丰富。目前已探明的矿产资源有12类35种,其中煤、石油、天然气、盐碱、高岭土等在全国占有重要地位。拥有全国1/6煤炭储量和良好的外运条件,决定了煤炭采掘最早成为扩张最快的资源开发项目。改革开放初期国营、集体、个体兴办的大、中、小型煤矿星罗棋布,使伊克昭盟这一昔日的"穷乡僻壤"迅速成为远近知名的投资胜地。随后,经过规模化、机械化、自动化和清洁环保为标准的重组整合,煤炭生产的工艺技术、安全环保和经济效益都达到国内同行业甚至国际上的先进水平。

以"资源换产业"接续发展

单纯的资源开发在经济学意义上只有增长,没有发展。只有把关联产业配套兴办起来,才能实现经济繁荣、社会发展、人民富裕。然而,"资金随开矿而来,又随原料外运而走"的空转现象很快引起人们的深刻反思。典型的教训全世界皆有。远的有美国"西进运动"中形成的矿区城镇不久即大量衰败,近的有国内多个开矿几十年的资源型城市难以为继。更具有强烈对比意义的是,不少资源输出国以贫穷为结局,而靠资源输入的亚洲四小龙及日本却成功地实现了"经济起飞"。有鉴于此,"煤炭就地转化比例"、"高端产业优先配给资源"成为各地引进企业和项目的先决条件。不断延伸产业链的结果,使鄂尔多斯已成为全国重要的煤化工基地、火电及可再生电力基地、盐碱化工基地、多种原材料基地。机械制造业和云计算代表的电子信息产业也正在形成规模化发展态势。

以"宜居宜业城市"博取永续发展

随着资源的深度开发和产业的拓展延伸，大规模兴办的企业需要改善经营管理的环境条件和公共服务，大量聚集的人口需要城市功能的支撑。然而，鄂尔多斯市周边过去就已经形成了比较密集的城市圈。在距离中心城区 500 公里范围内百万人口以上的大城市就有 10 来个，而且千万人口级的世界城市——北京也在这一空中距离内。在资源开发初期，大型企业一般都愿意把生产场所设在当地，而把管理机构和经营团队驻在外地大城市。显然，这种模式不利于资源高效转化和经济持续发展。只有通过宜居宜业的城市环境条件吸引和留住人气，在资源开发地区最大限度完成产业链的延伸和消费规模的扩大，才能实现高效、全面、环保、持久的发展。在这方面，德国鲁尔矿区的转型提供了成功范例。从 20 世纪 60 年代开始，鲁尔区通过产业结构调整和生态城市建设，把已经衰败的煤炭钢铁基地建设成为产业多元、环境优美、景色秀丽的城市群。在 4600 平方公里范围内，现在拥有 5 万人口以上的城市 24 个，支撑了重化工业、轻工业、旅游服务和文化产业的共同发展，创造了德国 40% 的工业产值。核心城市埃森市昔日是欧洲最大的煤城，如今则是众多国际性集团企业的驻地，2010 年获得"欧洲文化之都"称号，人口达到 62 万人，成为德国第六大城市。自觉主动地借鉴德国鲁尔矿区衰败的教训和经验，就是要防止"衰而后生"的曲折在鄂尔多斯重演。

三、构建"资源—产业—城市"同步发展的格局

改革开放初期，当时的伊克昭盟除了个别新建工厂外，基本没有现代化产业可言。30 多年后的现在，几乎所有工业生产都采用了现代先进的工艺技术

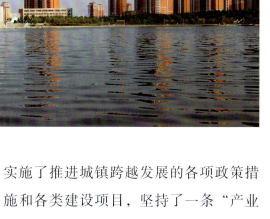

和设备。现有年产值 10 亿元以上的企业 124 家,年产值 100 亿元以上的企业 17 家,营业收入超百亿元的工业园区 6 个。2012 年全市地区生产总值达到 3657 亿元,财政收入达到 820 亿元,其中地方收入 376 亿元。与此同时,城镇化率从 1978 年的 10.5% 提高到 2012 年的 72%。当年的盟府所在地东胜县城关镇总人口 10 万人。现在,中心城区已经形成"东胜—康巴什—阿勒腾席热"三大组团,其中仅东胜区城镇人口达到 56 万人,增长约 4 倍多。

实施主动型城镇化战略

工业化和城镇化是一对孪生兄弟。但是作为后发地区而言,必须改变被动跟进的城镇化路线,以适度超前来弥补现实中已存在的滞后,才有可能为经济、社会和生态环境的全面建设提供龙头带动和空间支撑。特别是在本世纪撤盟设市后的十多年内,鄂尔多斯不失时机地实施了推进城镇跨越发展的各项政策措施和各类建设项目,坚持了一条"产业支撑,规划统领,基础先行,特色取胜,政府主导,市场运作"的正确路径。

高标准设定城市发展目标

充分发挥拆迁量较小。建设成本较低、资金筹集渠道较多、经济发展迅猛的优势,把城市目标锁定在满足长远发展的基础之上。

现代服务功能完善。适应多元化的要求,满足各类人群创业、就业、居家、出行、教育、医疗、文化、娱乐的现实和长远需要。

生态环境良好。通过防沙治沙、营造林带、建设生态绿地广场、严格防治污染等工程项目,保护生态环境的自然性和安全性。现在建成区绿化覆盖率达到 40.5%,人均公园绿地面积达到 29 平方米。

"住有所居"远近兼顾。应顾及不

同层次居民对"功能完善、设施齐全、环境优美"的住房要求。对低收入家庭的住房保障，也要从临时救助和长远发展两个方面予以结合，并且高于通行标准。2012年鄂尔多斯市居民人均住房面积已达到41.8平方米。

营造地域与民族特色。 如何在"千城一面"的流行顽症中脱颖而出，需要探索，更需要实践。鄂尔多斯有条件充分利用自然、历史、民族文化中提炼的各种元素，着力打造"自然环境长出来的城市"、"历史长河推出来的城市"、"文化底蕴凝聚出来的城市"。这是现代文明的体现，也是提高城市竞争力的重要途径。

防止"城市病"。 交通拥堵、环境污染、住房短缺、教育与医疗缺乏、社会治安不良、贫民窟频现等统称的"城市病"过去大多在国外城市流行，近年却在我国的大多数城市不同程度地爆发。然而在鄂尔多斯市，这些"城市病"不仅现在得到有效预防，而且从已具备的条件看，将来也不会有存在的基础。随着法规政策的完善，完全可以实现远离"城市病"的健康持续发展。

以城带乡，一体化发展。 在推进公共服务、基本保障、社会事业均等化和户籍制度改革的同时，开展村镇体系规划，推进"村改居"、中心村庄、家庭牧场等各种类型的新农村、新牧区建设。

四、展望

对城市发展的预期可谓见仁见智。过去人们常常从一般经验出发设想西部资源型城市，认为不外乎是矿工云集之城；"淘金"者过客之城；偏远风沙之城；随矿兴衰的"短命"之城等等。然而，这些常规的预测已经被奇迹般的发展彻底粉碎。只要对鄂尔多斯稍有了解的人就会明白，这些都已经是过时的观念。

然而，在资源富集区要想真正形成"资源开发、产业构建、城市建设"同步发展的局面，实际上必须做到城市的超前规划、超常规建设才能补上"短板"。这就需要客观认识和处理一定时间内难以避免的"空城"、"空房"问题。

"空城"现象最早出现于西方的"蔓延型"城市。由于富裕起来的中产阶级追求宽敞的居住条件而迁移到郊区，随之城市中心区要么无人居住，要么贫困集中，成为流浪汉出没之地，因而谓之"鬼城"。我国改革开放以来，从率先对外开放的14个沿海城市开始，除个别特例之外，新规划区都出现过若干年的"空城"现象。本来中国人口众多的国情决定了论及城市必是"人头攒动"的景象，从无空城之虑。但是近年来国际上"唱衰"中国的论调时有流行，乐于将中国新建城区贴上"鬼城"的标签。鄂尔多斯市建设快，名气大，自然要处于争论的风口浪尖。然而最终的结论只能由经济、社会、城市能否持续发展来决定。事实上争论最热的康巴什新区2004年动工兴建，9年后的现在已有10万人工作和生活，如果在西方国家应当是人气最旺的新城了。

"空房"现象本来是全国性的房地产投机长期以来得不到有效遏制的产物。在鄂尔多斯市由于大量的社会闲置资金无序流入住房市场，因而住宅建设出现了爆发式的增加，一时间空置现象比较突出，于是持不同观点的解读者都试图以此来作为例证。就历史而论，住房制度的商品化、社会化改革是解决计划经济时期因福利分房造成严重缺房问题的根本途径。但是，无节制的过度投机却违背了住房是特殊商品的基本属性，客观规律之手进行调节也是必然要发生的。调整的过程则取决于"无形之手"——市场要素的互动和"有形之手"——政策法规的完善。就全国地级市而言，鄂尔多斯市的"空房"总量并不是最多的，建造成本和价位相对较低，调整所需的时间应该也不会很长。

鄂尔多斯市的经济、社会和城镇发展都已经处于一个全新的基础之上。只要当地资源开发与全国经济增长的紧密联系不变，只要综合发展、可持续发展的指导方针不变，城市兴旺发达的动力就不会减弱。持续健康发展的现代生态宜居城市将不断出现在内蒙古高原。

Introduction

"Urban haze" becomes a hot topic in and out of China; people are now longing worse for white clouds on the blue sky and shining stars in the evening. However, after looking around all the cities, we would find out that only in Highland City can we enjoy a clear and natural modern living environment. Ordos, a city 500km away to Beijing shares a preeminent position due to its pure environment and great altitude which is more than one thousand meters.

One. Livable environment on thousand-meter altitude

In modern times, plain cities, coastal cities and those in the middle and lower reaches of the rivers are all suffering from a common persistent ailment—air, water and soil pollution are now worse and worse; especially in those countries with a high population density, that is why livable environment are moving up to the cities on higher ground.

Livability returning to the high terrain is historical trends

In Stone Age, Plateau regions were best living places for ancient human to get away from floods and transgression, to collect a wide variety of flora and fauna and to manufacture a large number of tools. Ancient site built in ten thousand years ago in our country including Yunnan Yuanmou, Beijing Zhoukoudian site, Shaanxi Lantian, Dayao site in Inner Mongolia, Zhalainuoer, Salawusu and Ulanmulun site are all placed at higher altitudes. Advantage of plains gradually revealed after agricultural civilization emerged, when Cities and villages turned out to be on the alluvial plains. Industrial civilization and The Age of Great Discovery in last several centuries contributed to the construction of coastal port cities. However,

这些常规的预测已经被奇迹般的发展彻底粉碎。只要对鄂尔多斯稍有了解的人就会明白，这些都已经是过时的观念。

然而，在资源富集区要想真正形成"资源开发、产业构建、城市建设"同步发展的局面，实际上必须做到城市的超前规划、超常规建设才能补上"短板"。这就需要客观认识和处理一定时间内难以避免的"空城"、"空房"问题。

"空城"现象最早出现于西方的"蔓延型"城市。由于富裕起来的中产阶级追求宽敞的居住条件而迁移到郊区，随之城市中心区要么无人居住，要么贫困集中，成为流浪汉出没之地，因而谓之"鬼城"。我国改革开放以来，从率先对外开放的14个沿海城市开始，除个别特例之外，新规划区都出现过若干年的"空城"现象。本来中国人口众多的国情决定了论及城市必是"人头攒动"的景象，从无空城之虑。但是近年来国际上"唱衰"中国的论调时有流行，乐于将中国新建城区贴上"鬼城"的标签。鄂尔多斯市建设快、名气大，自然要处于争论的风口浪尖。然而最终的结论只能由经济、社会、城市能否持续发展来决定。事实上争论最热的康巴什新区2004年动工兴建，9年后的现在已有10万人工作和生活，如果在西方国家应当是人气最旺的新城了。

"空房"现象本来是全国性的房地产投机长期以来得不到有效遏制的产物。在鄂尔多斯市由于大量的社会闲置资金无序流入住房市场，因而住宅建设出现了爆发式的增加，一时间空置现象比较突出，于是持不同观点的解读者都试图以此来作为例证。就历史而论，住房制度的商品化、社会化改革是解决计划经济时期因福利分房造成严重缺房问题的根本途径。但是，无节制的过度投机却违背了住房是特殊商品的基本属性，客观规律之手进行调节也是必然要发生的。调整的过程则取决于"无形之手"——市场要素的互动和"有形之手"——政策法规的完善。就全国地级市而言，鄂尔多斯市的"空房"总量并不是最多的，建造成本和价位相对较低，调整所需的时间应该也不会很长。

鄂尔多斯市的经济、社会和城镇发展都已经处于一个全新的基础之上。只要当地资源开发与全国经济增长的紧密联系不变，只要综合发展、可持续发展的指导方针不变，城市兴旺发达的动力就不会减弱。持续健康发展的现代生态宜居城市将不断出现在内蒙古高原。

Introduction

"Urban haze" becomes a hot topic in and out of China; people are now longing worse for white clouds on the blue sky and shining stars in the evening. However, after looking around all the cities, we would find out that only in Highland City can we enjoy a clear and natural modern living environment. Ordos, a city 500km away to Beijing shares a preeminent position due to its pure environment and great altitude which is more than one thousand meters.

One. Livable environment on thousand-meter altitude

In modern times, plain cities, coastal cities and those in the middle and lower reaches of the rivers are all suffering from a common persistent ailment—air, water and soil pollution are now worse and worse; especially in those countries with a high population density, that is why livable environment are moving up to the cities on higher ground.

Livability returning to the high terrain is historical trends

In Stone Age, Plateau regions were best living places for ancient human to get away from floods and transgression, to collect a wide variety of flora and fauna and to manufacture a large number of tools. Ancient site built in ten thousand years ago in our country including Yunnan Yuanmou, Beijing Zhoukoudian site, Shaanxi Lantian, Dayao site in Inner Mongolia, Zhalainuoer, Salawusu and Ulanmulun site are all placed at higher altitudes. Advantage of plains gradually revealed after agricultural civilization emerged, when Cities and villages turned out to be on the alluvial plains. Industrial civilization and The Age of Great Discovery in last several centuries contributed to the construction of coastal port cities. However,

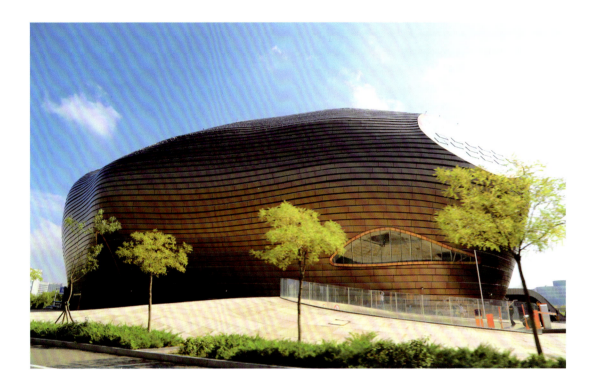

when human step into Information technology and post-industrial era, environment, resources, economy, social condition which constituting livability need to be redefined, as a result, cities in highlands begin to show their advantages on environment and resources. Two most famous new-built cities in the later Half of the 20th century -- Brasilia and Chandigarh are located in high elevations.

Continental climate blocks Asian Brown Cloud

Originated in the North India Ocean, Asian Brown Cloud discovered in 1999, it only affected subcontinent of South Asia and Southeast Asia at that time. However, Cloud's thickness has amounted to several kilometers due to the intensification of the predisposing factors including Industrial and traffic emissions, straw burning, forest and grass fires, volcanic eruptions and so on in last dozen years; the influenced areas spread not only to the southern Asia and east of the entire maritime region any longer, but also affected the western North America and northern Africa. Astronauts said that there were less blue but more blur on the earth can be seen from the international space station. Anyway, Plateau with continental climate is beyond the recurrent drift range of "Asian brown cloud", and that is why these places can always live with fresh airs.

Area layout being forced to adjust by fine particulate pollution

In recent year, Cities carry out air pollution control with the dust (PM10: pollutant particles with a diameter less than 10 microns) being index, most of the conclusion indicated that fine days were increasing. But the decline in total amount of airborne dust on the surface does not mean substantially released the pollution degree, because the constitution of Contaminants worsened. The continuous increased proportion caused by combustion emissions, vehicle exhaust, and industrial evaporation and drifting fine particles across the regions made haze getting worse and worse in urban areas. Especially in winter and spring the reality is that hazes come one by one extremely close in coastal cities and plains, which drives people to concern more about fine particles "haze" then larger particles. In the wave against haze, it is really necessary to carry out comprehensive adjustment and optimization on industrial layout, energy structure, urban functions and environmental standards. It has been put on the agenda to transfer resource-based industries to the vicinity of raw materials and to shift energy producing industries to energy-rich regions. Regions with environmental capacity, strong self-purification and rich renewable energy should seek for chance to develop as well as take the responsibilities to adjust. It is really a right time to construct modern livable cities on higher grounds.

Advantage of building livable environment in Ordos

Ordos sits in the convergence zone where continental climate meets oceanic climate. In terms of central city, all the environmental conditions are suitable, moderate and easy to avoid disadvantages.

Moderate elevation: elevation of 1100-1400m above the sea level finely helps to build a pressure suitable, oxygen adequate condition which is conducive to human health.

Suitable temperature: The annual average day temperature (maximum) is about 12 degree, and seasons here are distinct and comfortable without extremely cold or hot in winter and summer.

Appropriate Humidity: three side of this city are surrounded by Yellow River, with tributaries spreading, average annual rainfall here reaches 390mm, and monthly humidity is generally between 40% and 60%.

Adequate sunlight: average annual sunshine-hour is about 3,100 hours, with a sunshine ratio of 70%, just like a "sunny bar".

Fine Air Mobility: central city area is in an open and flat undulating plateau, without any Mountains or sand dunes blocking off. Annual average wind speed is about 3.5m / s, while about 4.5 m / s in April when sandstorm occurs, northwest winds accounts most. These characters can not only resist the invasive "brown cloud" pollution form eastern coast, but also help to maintain the fresh air in urban areas.

Diverse Biology: soil in urban area is good to the growth of various plants with a average accumulated temperature up to 2800 °C. There are sand prairie, typical steppe, desert steppe and desert lakeside meadow; conditions for vegetation and ecological restoration are wonderful. Generally, there is little pollution in air, soil and groundwater, so all kinds of organic and pollution-free animals and plants can be feed and produced in local places.

There are 25 elderly people who is more than 100 years, some banners even nearly catch up with longevities which share a rate of 7.5 per ten-thousandths. This is a profile which shows the coordinated development of economic society and urban constructions; also the potential of being a livable place in Ordos is now being discovered, and doing goods to the citizens.

Two. Livable city out of "resource curse"

The reform and opening up policy pushed

Ordos with rich research and superior location to the forefront of development and construction in 1980s, right at the time when "resource depletion" and "resource curse" occurred in and out of China forced people to make a decision on how to achieve coordinated development and sustainable development.

So-called "resource curse", is simply caused by explicate large numbers of natural resources at once and supplant other develop elements, thus stifled opportunities for long-term development and finally ended up with poverty and ruins in resource origins due to the outflow of raw materials, vest and population. One of the efficient way to break this curse is to build a new structure which stress on resource development, industrial development and building livable cities at the same time.

Start development by "resources for capital"

Ground and underground resources in Ordos are very abundant; there are already 35 kinds of minerals in 12 classifications founded so far; coal, soil, natural gas, salt and kaolin occupy important positions in the country. Coal mining is the first developing program since there are 1/6 Coal Reserves and good Sinotrans conditions. At the early stage of reform and opening up, coalmines in all sizes initiate by country, collectivity and individual spread all around; this made Ih Ju League get away from backward place into a famous place to invest. After that, safety and environmental protection, technology and economic efficiency of coal mining here reach the country advanced level in the same industry, even international level, thanks to the reorganization and integration in the standard of large-scale, mechanization, automation and environmental.

Continue developing by "resources for industry"

Simple resource development means only growing and no developing in the economic sense. A city can only realize economic prosperity, social development and people's rich when related supporting industries were set up. However, people begin to rethink hardly by the Idling phenomenon which funding comes along with the mining but goes with the raw materials. Typical lessons are worldwide: mining towns formed in "Westward Movement" declined soon in USA while several resource-based cities in China built decades ago are unsustainable any more. Ironically, the Four Tigers of Asia and Japan are resource-inputting countries; they are succeeding in economic take-off while many resource-exporting countries are ended up with poverty. In view of this, "proportion of coal conversing locally" and "high-end industries priority rationing resources" became a precondition for all regions to introduce enterprises and projects. Thanks to extending industrial chain, Ordos has become a national key foundation of Coal Chemical industry, thermal power and renewable electricity, alkali salt and many other raw materials. IT industry represented by machinery manufacturing and cloud computing is now seeking its position here.

Gain sustainable development by Livable and Enterprise-adaptable cities

With the extension of industries and further exploitation of resources, enterprises in large scale need to improve their public services and environmental conditions of operation and management while large concentration of population needs the support of urban functions. Nevertheless, surroundings of Ordos had already formed intensive urban circles once.

There are nearly 10 cities with a population more than a million at a distance of 500 kilometers to the city center, Beijing—a world city with more than 10 million citizens is also within such an air distance. At the early stage of resource development, most large enterprises are willing to set up workplace in local places, but administration and management team in nonlocal cities. Apparently, this model does no good to efficient transformation of resources and sustainable economic development. Efficient, comprehensive, environmental, sustained development can only be realized if livable environment conditions can attract and retain popularity, while maximum expansion of industrial chain and extension of consumption scale could be completed in resource exploited areas. In term of this, transformation of Germany's Ruhr mining provides a successful example. Since the 1960s Ruhr constructed declined steel base into a beautiful and scenic city group with diverse industries by adjusting industrial structure and constructing ecologic city. Now, there are 24 cities with over 50,000 residents in a range within 4600 km^2, which great support the joint development of heavy industry, light industry, tourism services and cultural industries and create 40% of industrial output in Germany. Core city--Essen was once Europe's largest coal city, today it is one of the seat of many international conglomcrates. In 2010, Essen gains a name of Capital of European Culture, with 620,000 citizens and being the sixth largest city in Germany. Ordos should avoid any repeat of rising after declined by consciously learn lessons and experiences of Ruhr.

Three. Construct simultaneous development pattern of "resource-city-

industry"

At The beginning of reform and opening up, there were barely modern industries expect several new-built enterprises. Now 30 years later, nearly all the industrial productions adopted advanced technology and equipment. There are 124 companies with annual output value of one billion Yuan, 17 enterprises with annual output value of 10 billion Yuan, and 6 industrial park with a operating income over ten billion Yuan. In 2012, total output value in the whole city amounted 365.7 billion Yuan, and revenue reached 82 billion Yuan among which 37.6 billion Yuan are local revenue. Meanwhile, urbanization rate increased from 10.5% in 1978 to 72% in 2012. Total population in Chengguan town in Dongsheng—where the league office sit at that tome is 100 thousand; but now there are 560 thousand residents in only urban area of Dongsheng due to the central city have been consisted by group of "Dongsheng-Kangbashi- Ale Tengxire", almost increased by 4 times.

Implementing active urbanization strategy

Industrialization and urbanization are twins. But as a backward area, Ordos need to change the passive urbanization route in order to make up the backward which is already existing, then overall construction on economic, social and eco-environment could be offered with leading and space supports. Especially in the ten years after "league to city", Ordos took its chance to implement all kinds of policies and a construction to promote urbanization, by stick on the right way which is "industry support, planning guide, foundation goes first and wins by features, government-led, market operation".

Setting development goal in high standard

Urban goal need to be locked on the base of long-term development by taking advantages of little demolition, low cost of construction, rich channel of fund raising and rapid economic development.

Improving modern service functions. Urban functions need to meet the need of diversification, and meet the requirements of all kinds of people on the Entrepreneurship, employment, home, travel, education, health, culture and entertainment.

Pretty ecologic environment, Ordos tries to protect maturity and safety of eco-environment by engineering projects like desertification, forest construction, building ecological green square and strict pollution control. Now the green coverage ratio in completed area is 40.5% with per capita green area being $29m^2$.

Considering exhaustive to make sure everyone has a house to live in. all residential area in different level need to meet the requirement of Perfect function, complete facilities, beautiful environment. Even the Housing security for low-income families, house need to consider current demand and long-term development at the same time and be higher than standard. per capita housing area in urban areas has reached $41.8m^2$ in 2012.

Creating local and ethnic characteristics. It needs more exploration and practice to make a city outstanding in thousands of cities. Ordos tries to build "a city born in nature", "city found in the river of history" and "city comes out form deep culture" by taking advantages from all elements in nature, history and ethnic culture.

preventing the "urban diseases": urban diseases like traffic jam, environment pollution, housing shortage, education and medicine shortage, bad social security and slums are popular mostly in foreign countries, but now, they begin to emerge in most countries in China. However, in Ordos these urban diseases are not only been avoided, but also be out of consideration in the future in term of equipment existing. With the completion of policies and laws, Ordos can totally realize sound and sustained development without urban diseases.

Integrated development with urban driving village. All constructions of building New countryside and new pastoral area in villages, central towns and prairies with a systemic regulation, at the same time

when promoting public services, Basic Protection, social programs qualify and reform of household registration system.

Four. Prospect

Everyone has his own idea about the prospect of urban development. In the past, people always think about western resource-based cities with common experiences, and take there as cities where miners gathered and gold rusher traveled, and cities where sand and wind covered. Normal prediction has now been crushed by the magical development. Once you know Ordos even for a little bit, you would know those are notions out of time.

However, if Ordos really wants to create a complexion that resource development, industrial construction develop together with city construction in regions with rich resources, it need to achieve advance planning and Ultra conventional buildings first to make up the shortage; and that will take a while to recognize and deal with some problems like empty city and empty house which could not be avoid in a short of time.

Empty city first appeared in spread type cities in western. The rich middle class moves to outskirts since they chased for spacious living conditions, as a result, central cities were either uninhabited or gathered poor and being places of wanderer. That is the origin of "Ghost town". Since the reform and opening up in our country, except individual exceptions, empty city occurred in each new-built district in the 14 coastal cities. Originally, there would be no empty city in our country because of the large population, and urban areas should be crowd. But in recent years, many reports out of China try to tag "Ghost town" on Chinese new-built towns. Ordos enjoys a great fame because of its rapid development, so it would naturally be in the forefront of debate; nevertheless, the final conclusion depends on the economic, social and sustainable development in this city. In fact, the hottest topic—new district in Kangbashi built in 2004, has a population more the 100,000, being a most popular new city while comparing with western cities.

The phenomenon of empty house is the product of real estate speculation which has never been controlled for a long time in the whole country. Residential buildings are increased in Ordos because large amount of social idle funds flowed into housing market without any regulation and it would be empty for a short time; that caused audiences with different understandings try to make this as an outstanding example. From the point view of history, commercialization of residential house and reform of socialization are the basic solution to deal with the problem caused by welfare-oriented public housing distribution system in planned economy period. However, immoderate over speculation go against to the basic nature of housing being special commodity, that is why it is necessary to adjust by objective law. Procedure of adjustment depends on the interaction of invisible hands--market factors as well as visible hand—completed policy and law. In terms of the cities in our country, the amount of empty house in Ordos is not the most, so it would not take long to adjust since the cost of construction and the selling-price is really low.

Economy, social and urban development in Ordos is now on the totally new base. The power for this city to be thriving would never reduce in only local resource development connected tightly with national economic growth, and the guidelines of comprehensive and sustainable development maintains. There would be more and more livable cities developed Sustainable and healthily in Inner Mongolia like Ordos.

第一章

应势而城

Chapter One

City out of Complexion

"鄂尔多斯"蒙古语原意为"众多宫帐",后来专指在当地游牧生产生活和保卫成吉思汗祭灵宫帐的蒙古部落。现在还是一些自然、历史、经济、社会方面重大成就的专有冠名。2001年"盟改市"后成为地级市域的名称。

1. "鄂尔多斯盆地"造就资源富集区

以"鄂尔多斯"命名的这一中国第二大沉积盆地位于吕梁山以西、秦岭以北、贺兰山以东、阴山以南,总面积达30多万平方公里。鄂尔多斯市7万多平方公里的行政辖区位于该盆地北部,是煤炭、天然气、石油等多种矿藏的集中分布区域。2012年鄂尔多斯市的煤炭产量达6.3亿吨,占全国产量的1/6;管道天然气输送到周边各大城市和首都北京;所产众多门类的原材料成为国家建设的重要物质基础。依托大型、集群矿区所建设的工业园区、工矿城镇和中小城市推动了全市域快速城镇化的浪潮。

2. "鄂尔多斯人"开启当地人类史研究

1923年,一位法国古生物学家在萨拉乌素遗址(今鄂尔多斯市乌审旗境内,距今14—7万年)发现了古人类化石,"Ordos Man"(鄂尔多斯人)得以问世。后来我国的考古学家依照鄂尔多斯地区外围三面环绕黄河"几"字形弯曲的"河套"古称,将这一古人类冠名为"河套人"。进一步的研究证明"河套人"在中国乃至世界人类进化史链条上具有独特意义。随后考古发现的水洞沟、朱开沟、阳湾及多处古长城、秦直道、历代墓葬、窖藏等众多遗址表明,鄂尔多斯地区具有石器时代、青铜器时代、铁器时代及华夏各朝代连续的人类文化更替遗迹。特别是大量出土的青铜器、金器及丰富的史料表明,鄂尔多斯数千年以来一直是人类活动的重要舞台,也是草原文明和农耕文明的交汇繁荣之地。2010年在中心城区新发现的乌兰木伦遗址出土了3400多件人工打制石器、4200多件动物化石和大量的骨制品及用火遗迹。这一重大考古成果进一步弥补了这一区域人类进化史上距今4~7万年的链条。而且在沿乌兰木伦河70公里的两岸区域发现了80多处石器分布点。揭示了古人类在鄂尔多斯地区繁衍栖息的连续性和密集程度。

3. "鄂尔多斯高原"独具地缘和环境优势

黄土高原和内蒙古高原在这里交汇。地理位置便于南下关中、东赴大洋、北连欧亚草原大通道，无论是对古人类文明演进，还是对当代经济社会发展都具有十分有利的条件。"高原"所决定的自然属性还在环境保护和生态文明建设中具有独特的优越条件。

4. 持续不断的古代建城史

人群的聚集必然形成村落和城池。考古和史料都证明，从春秋战国以来鄂尔多斯一直是城池众多的地区。早在两千多年前秦朝从首都咸阳城到边关九原城（今包头市境内）的"直道"上及附近地区就有好几处名称见诸于古籍的城池。秦汉两朝在今鄂尔多斯地区设立了郡和县，有些城池遗址尚存至今。如西河郡治所之一霍洛柴登古城遗址东西长 1446 米，南北宽 1100 米，夯筑墙体最宽处达 13 米。城内的官署及炼铁、炼铜、铸币、铸兵器等场所现在仍可清晰辨认。汉代的美稷县城后来还充当过南匈奴的单于庭（首都）。公元 5 世纪初匈奴铁弗部"天王大单于"赫连勃勃以"大河套"为中心建立大夏国（史称胡夏），所建都城名为统万城，据说意在"统领万邦"。城市格局仿照汉朝首都，由宫城、内城、外城三部分构成，是驰骋欧亚草原近千年的匈奴（匈人）留存至今的唯一城市遗址。现存于乌审旗南缘的这座城廓仍清晰可见，角楼遗迹高达 30 多米。十二连城则是由明朝以前几个朝代先后兴建的十二座古城所组成。隋炀帝曾在此会盟各民族首领，为统一北方草原和西域地区发挥了政治中心作用。明朝时在此设东胜右卫，成为与北元蒙古政权发生军事、政治、经济关系的重要场所。

5. 草原移动之城——成吉思汗祭灵白宫

成吉思汗于 1227 年逝世后，蒙古大汗在漠北设"白色宫帐"祭祀。后来在元上都（今内蒙古正蓝旗境内）、元大都（今北京）都设立过祭祀宫殿。15 世纪中叶之后，祭祀成吉思汗的"八白宫帐"固定在鄂尔多斯。每年举行的几十次专项祭奠和定时祭奠都有专门程式和丰富内容。特别是大祭时，蒙古包连片，人群聚集，规模宏大。1956 年成吉思汗陵园建成，移动祭祀宫帐改为固定宫殿，并且将过去一些分散的祭物集中在陵园中祭祀。21 世纪初陵园进行扩建，增建了旅游展览区和居民新区，围绕成吉思汗祭祀和蒙元文化形成了一个传统和现代有机结合的新城镇。同时，成吉思汗史料及蒙元文化成为鄂尔多斯塑造城市风貌的重要元素。

Ordos, it means "lots of Palace tent", which latterly referred to Mongolian groups who were nomadic and protecting sacrifice tent of Genghis Khan. Now it is also a special title of great achievements on natural, historic, economical and social fields. In 2001, it formally became a name of prefecture-level city after "League to City".

One. Resource-rich Regions Made by Ordos Basin

The second largest sedimentary basin of china named "Ordos" locates to the west of Lvliang Mount, east of Helan mount and south of Yinshan Mount, with a total area more than 300,000 km^2.The jurisdictions more than 70,000 km^2 of Ordos is in the northern basin, being an concentrated distribution area of mineral deposits including coal, natural gas and petroleum. In 2010, coal output in Ordos reached 630 milliom tons, accounting 1/6 of the country's total output; pipeline gas are sent to neighboring cities and the capital. Beside, many raw materials produce in Ordos are important supports of nation-building. Urbanization in this area has been largely promoted by the industrial parks, mining towns and small sized cities built on the large mining Cluster.

Two. Local Human History Research Led by "Ordos Man"

In 1923, a French paleontologist discovered ancient human fossils at the Sala WuSu site (now in the Uxin Banner of Ordos, with an age about 70,000-140,000 years), and then Ordos man came out of earth. Later, archaeologists named these ancient men "Hetao Man" after Ω-shaped Hetao (bend of a river) of Yellow River which covered three sides of Ordos. After future research, Hetao Man was proven extremely important in the chain of human evolution of China, even of the whole worldNumerous sites discovered laterly include Shuidonggou, ZhuKaigou, Yangwan and others like acient Great Wall, Qin Straight Road, ancient tomb and hoarding, they all indicate that Ordos remains linked relics of human culture replacement during the stone age, the bronze age, the iron age and each dynasty in China. In particular, a large number of unearthed bronze, gold vessels and rich historic date show that Ordos is an important place of human activities as well as a prosperous land for intersection of farming civilization and prairie culture. There are more than 3,400 artificial stone implement, over 4,200 pieces of animal bone fossils, large amount of bone products and traces of fire were unearthed in 2010 at newfound Ulanmulun site in the central Ordos. This great archaeological achievement has made up the date of human evolution for nearly 40,000 to 70,000 years in this field. What is more, there are more than 80 distributions of stone implement on the 70km bank region beside the Ulammulun River, which indicated the continuous and intensive degree of ancient human in Ordos.

Three. Unique Geography& Environmental Advantages of Ordos Plateau

Inner Mongolia plateau meets the Loess Plateau here, in this case, with Shuanxi to the south, ocean to the east and Eurasian steppe corridor to the north, its shares a favorable condition to contemporary economic and social development as well as civilization progress of ancient human. Natural attributes made by "plateau" also enjoys a unique advantage in environment protection and ecological civilization.

Four. Continuous History of Ancient City

Where is human being, there are villages and fortresses. Archaeological and historical data have proven that Ordos has been a region with lots of cities since Spring and Autumn and Warring States Period. Dating back to two thousand years ago in Qin Dynasty, there were already several cities recorded on the ancient books, which sited in the areas from Straight Road in Jiuyuan city (now in Baotou city) to Changan the capital. There were counties settled in Ordos in Qin and Han Dynasty, some are even survived to today, including Huoluocaideng site in Xihe County which is 1,446m from east and west, 1100m from south to north with a 13-meter ramming wall. Now, we can still clearly identify government offices and places for iron and copper smelting, mintage and weapon casting. Mei Ji County in Han Dynasty later changed into Chanyu court (capital) of South Huns. In the early fifth Century, the "Great Chanyu King" of Teflon Huns named Helian Bobo built the Great Xia (recorded as Huxia) around the "Great Hetao", its capital was named Tongwan City which meant "commanding all the countries".

Structure of Tongwan City imitated to that of Han dynasty which is consisted of three parts: inner city, outer city and palace; and it is now the only city site made by Huns who occupied the Eurasian steppe for nearly thousand years. This city site can still be seen clearly in the south of Uxin Banner, with a turret up to 30 meters. Twelve linked cities are composed by twelve ancient cities built in different periods in several dynasties before Ming Dynasty. Emperor Yang of the Sui Dynasty had formed meetings here with leaders of other nations, which played a political center for unifying grasslands in northern and western areas. In Ming dynasty, Dongsheng imperial bodyguard was set here, and was a vital place to deal with military, political and economic relations with Post-imperial Mongolia regime.

Five. Moving city on the prairie—white Mourning Palace of Genghis Khan

After the death of Genghis Khan in 1227, Mongolia Khan set up a white palace in Mobei for worship ceremony. Later, mourning palaces were set up in Upper Capital of the Yuan (now called Zhenglan Banner) and the Capital (now Beijing). Since the Mid-15th century, Eight White Mourning Palace memorizing Genghis Khan was fixed in Ordos. There are dozens of Special festivals and Regular festivals every year with particular procedure and rich content. Especially during the big day of worshiping, continuous yurts covered a large scale with gathering crowds. New Mausoleum of Genghis Khan was completed in 1956 and changed moving mourning tent into a fixed palace, which can collete the scattered immolation in this cemetery for ritual sacrifices. Cemetery was extended at the beginning of this century, adding a tourism exhibition area and a resident district, and thus forms a new town of organic combination of traditional and modern with the core of Genghis Khan Worship and the Mongol-Yuan cultures. Meanwhile, historic date of Genghis Khan and Mongol-Yuan culture are the vital elements for shaping splendor of Ordos.

一、黄河围合的资源宝库
Resources Enclosed by Yellow River

鄂尔多斯市富含煤炭、天然气、石油及其他多种矿藏。黄河干流围绕三面，一级支流覆盖全境。矿产与水源同处一地的优势举世罕见。

黄河流经西部平原
Yellow River flowing through Western Plains

一级支流无定河流经南部沙地
Wuding River— First-grade Tributary of Yellow River Flowing Through Southern Sandlot

黄河流经东部丘陵
Yellow River Passing over Upland Eastern China

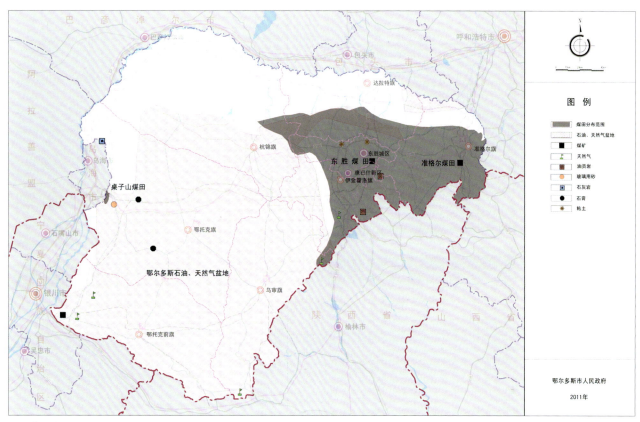

鄂尔多斯市矿产资源分布
Mineral Wealth Distribution in Ordos

巴图湾水库
Bartle Bay Reservoir

City out of Complexion | 29

二、多彩的自然生态
Various Natural Ecology

丘陵 Hills

沙地 Sandlot

沙漠 Sandlot/desert

草原 Prairie

湖泊 Lakes

湿地 Wetlands

三、远古人类聚集
Issues About the Ancient

商代民族分布
Ethnic Distribution in Shang Dynasty

距今 7-3 万年的乌兰木伦遗址
Ulanmulun Site built 70-30 Thousand-year ago

萨拉乌素遗址——距今 14-7 万年的河套人的栖息地
Salawusu site—Habitat of Loop Person 70-140 Thousand-year ago

寨子圪旦塔遗址
Zhaizigedan Tower Site

朱开沟遗址
Zhukaigou Site

四、古代文物遗存
Ancient Cultural Relics

鄂尔多斯市考古发现的青铜器、铁器、金银器、瓷器、绘画等证明草原文明和农耕文明交汇的历史变迁。

西夏牡丹纹酱釉剔花瓷瓶
Sauce Glazed Vase with Chiseled Peony of Hsihsia

匈奴金冠
Huns' Gold Headwear

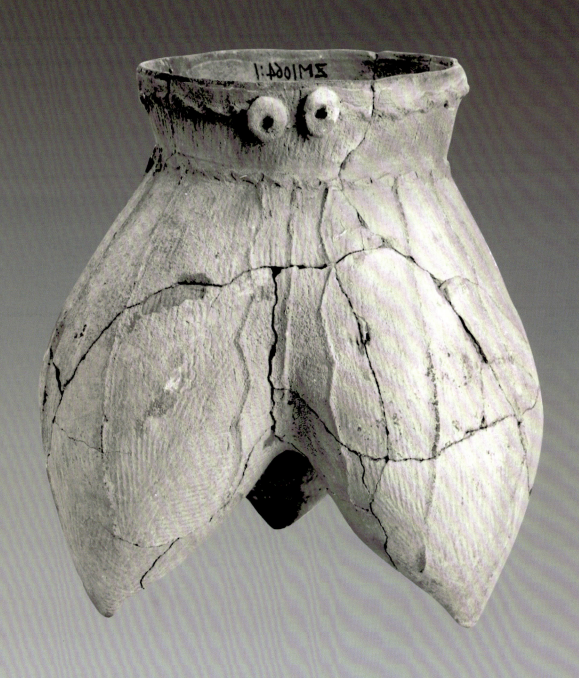

蛇纹陶鬲
The Serpentine Pottery

汉代铜漏
Han Dynasty Copper Drain

朱开沟遗址出土青铜短剑、刀
Bronze Half-sword and Sword Unearthed in Zhukaigou Site

盘角羊头形青铜辕头饰
Bronze headdress shaped as Argali sheep head

虎噬鹿纹青铜饰牌
Bronze Plate With Tiger Biting Deer

伫立鹿形青铜饰件
Standing deer-shaped bronze ornaments

汉代胡俑
Han Dynasty Pottery Figures

尖底陶瓶
V-bottom Pottery

唐代骑马俑
Tang Dynasty Pottery Figures on Horsebacks

City out of Complexion | 37

五、古代建城史
Ancient Building History

鄂尔多斯岩画 Ordos Cliff Painting

蒙古帝王受祭图 Mongolia Emperor being offered

汉代庭院图壁画 Han Dynasty Courtyard Mural

阿尔寨浮雕石塔 Arzhai Relief Spire

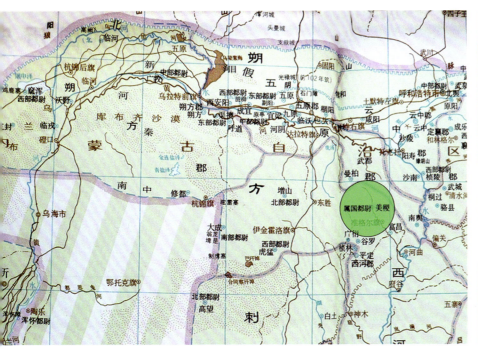

美稷城先后为汉代县城和南匈奴单于庭
Mei Ji City—Worked as Former county in Han Dynasty and Chanyu court in South Hsiungnu

十二连城 Twelve Linked-City

秦直道博物馆 Qin Straight Road Museum

依据史籍修建秦直道文化园 Qin Straight Road Cultural Park being built according historical records

统万城——铁弗匈奴所建大夏国都城遗址
Tongwan City—Site of Capital of Daxia Country built by Hsiungnu

六、成吉思汗陵的聚集效益
Aggregation Effect of Genghis Khan Mausoleum

游牧时代成吉思汗陵"八白宫"
Babai Palace—Mausoleum of Genghis Khan in Nomadic Era

20 世纪前期画家笔下的祭祀场景
Sacrificial Scene Under the brush in early 20th.

1956年落成的成吉思汗陵园成为弘扬民族文化的胜地
Mausoleum of Genghis Khan was built in 1956 as Shrine for propagating ethnic cultures.

每逢大祭人们不分远近、民族、身份齐集陵园，共同献上全羊、奶食、茶、酒等贡品
During the festival, people regardless of the distance, ethnic identity gathered in Cemetery and offered lamb, milk food, tea, wine and other tributes

煤电化工一体化基地
Integration Base of Chemical and Coal Industry

七、工业化带动城镇化
Industrialization Driving Urbanization

能源重化工基地
Base of Energy and Heavy Chemical Industry

现代化花园式煤矿
Modern garden type coal mine

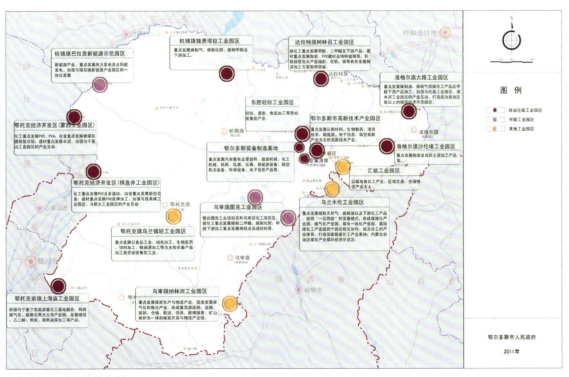

鄂尔多斯市产业结构规划（2011-2030）
The Ordos Industrial Structure Planning (2011-2030)

City out of Complexion | 45

西气东输集输站
Gathering station for West-East natural gas transmission project

西气东输净化厂
Purification plant for West-East natural gas transmission project

煤制油厂区夜景 Night in Coal Refinery

煤炭全封闭集装运输 All-enveloping container transport of coal

新建天然气田
Gas field

太阳能发电站
Solar power station

风力发电场 Wind Power Plant

煤化工循环经济园区 Circular economy park (cep) of coal chemical industry

八、特色旅游扩展城镇化
Tourism industry helps expanding urbanization

全市有国家级重点保护文物 12 处，自治区级重点保护文物 40 处，市级重点保护文物 51 处，旗（区）重点保护文物约 88 个，文化旅游产业成为城市化的新动力。

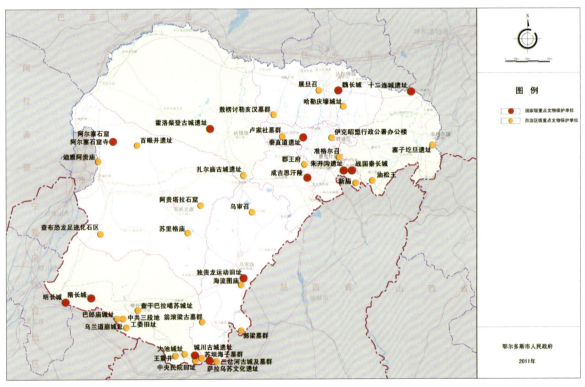

鄂尔多斯市历史与文化资源分布（2011–2030）
Distribution of cultural and historical resources in Ordos (2011–2030)

准格尔旗油松王景区 Pine King Scenic Spot in Jungar Banner

大沙头旅游景区 Dashatou tourist attraction

七星湖旅游景区 Seven Star Lake Scenic Spot

响沙湾旅游景区 Sand bay tourist attraction

沙雕 Sand sculpture

成吉思汗陵旅游景区 Genghis Khan Mausoleum Scenic Spot

恩格贝沙湖游览 Sandy Lake in Engebei

九、农牧业现代化支撑城镇化
Modernization of agriculture and animal husbandry in support of the Urbanization

温室农业
Greenhouse agricultural

大型喷灌机用于农田和草地灌溉
Irrigation machine for farmland and Grassland Irrigation

规模化现代农业 Scaled Modern agriculture

生态移民新社区 New community for ecological immigration

世界著名品种阿尔巴斯绒山羊 World famous Arbas Cashmere Goat

大型肉羊育肥基地 Large base for mutton sheep breeding

十、生态治理保障城镇化
Ecological management

小流域治理 Management of Small watershed

人工沙障固沙 Artificial sand barrier for sand-fixation

生态治理带动旅游 Ecological governance drives tourism

矿区复垦和绿化景观 Mine reclamation and landscape greening

退耕还林还草 Grain for green

沙漠治理一景 A view of Desert controlling

生态大道局部 Local Ecological Avenue

第二章

鄂尔多斯城市群

Chapter Two

Urban Agglomeration in Ordos

鄂尔多斯市（原伊克昭盟）位于内蒙古自治区西南部，2012年总人口196万，城镇化率达72%。市域总面积8.67万平方公里，地上地下资源都很丰富。其中70%地下蕴藏煤炭，素有"地下煤海"之称。

1. 城镇体系规划

根据《鄂尔多斯城镇体系规划》，全市域建成1个中心城市、2个副中心城市、10个重点镇、34个一般镇（苏木、乡）、18个重点产业园区，互相之间形成既合理分工又有机联系的发展格局。城镇对人口、要素的聚集、对全市域空间的辐射及对经济社会的支撑作用均达到国内较高水平。2015年市域总人口达到240万人左右，城镇化率达到80%；预计2030年总人口达到320万人左右，城镇化率可达93%左右。

城镇空间结构"一主两副四轴"。

一主：即由东胜—康巴什—阿镇三个组团构成的中心城区。既是能源、化工、羊绒服装、电子信息、机械制造生产基地，也是鄂尔多斯市的政治、经济、文化、交通中心。

两副：即薛家湾和树林召两个副中心城市。分别对接自治区的两个门户城市呼和浩特和包头。

四轴：包括在中心城区交叉的两条发展轴和环绕市域南北的两条发展轴。①包西发展轴：依托穿越南北的包头至西安铁路和高速公路、210国道沿线布局城镇和工业园区，向北对接自治区沿黄城市群并辐射蒙古国，向南对接陕西省并延伸南方各大城市，境内串联树林召、伊金霍洛、札萨克、乌兰木伦等城镇。②荣乌发展轴：依托穿越东西的荣城至乌海高速、109国道、东乌铁路，串联棋盘井、敖勒召其、锡尼、准格尔召、暖水等城镇。③沿黄河发展轴：依托京包兰综合运输通道和沿河高速，规划建设鄂托克旗蒙西、杭锦旗独贵塔拉、准格尔旗大路等工业园区。④沿边发展轴：依托南部交通干线，规划建设鄂托克前旗上海庙、乌审旗图克、伊金霍洛旗乌兰木伦等工业园区和旗中心镇，对接陕西、宁夏的相关城市。

在加快城镇建设的同时开展重点区域村镇体系规划，推进城乡统筹协调发展。

2. 区域合作

根据资源禀赋、区位条件、经济状况，鄂尔多斯在全区、省区际、全国发展格局中均居于重要位置。

内蒙古呼包鄂及沿黄城市群的重要增长极。 鄂尔多斯与呼和浩特市、包头市、巴彦淖尔市、乌海市、阿拉善盟隔黄河相望，现在已经通过多种交通接口连为一体，可以与相关城市优势互补，实现协调发展。

国家级呼包银榆经济区的核心地带。根据国务院正式批复的规划，该经济区的发展目标和几大产业的构建鄂尔多斯都将担当重要角色。特别是资源、产业、交通网高度重合的独特优势其他城市无法取代。该规划区内的8个民用机场除二连浩特机场稍远外，其他都位于鄂尔多斯市域周边，大部分城镇不出百公里就可以到达至少一个机场。在规划区邻省城市中西接银川进而向兰州方向辐射，南接榆林向延安—西安城市群辐射，有利于建立多元化、全方位的经济联系。

京津冀都市圈及环渤海城市群的重要侧翼。鄂尔多斯机场距首都机场空中距离500公里。市域东部距天津、秦皇岛港的公路、铁路距离600公里左右。产品外运、信息交流、人员旅行、国内外开放的区位条件都十分优越。

3. 交通网络

以区域枢纽机场为龙头，以城际铁路、干线铁路与高速公路为骨干，以干线公路与地方铁路公路为基础构建区域综合交通运输体系。在鄂尔多斯机场已经与众多国内城市通航的基础上继续增加航线，并建设各旗通勤机场。铁路运输提升运能，增强与外围铁路干线的沟通能力，形成"呼—包—鄂"城际铁路和"三横四纵"的铁路网。公路运输形成"井"字形高速公路网，建设"八横十二纵十一个省级出口二十七座黄河大桥"的密集网络。

4. 城镇与产业高度融合

以主副城市和四条发展轴线为重点，科学合理规划各类产业园区。其中，既有综合型园区，也有煤化工、原材料、机械制造、云计算（电子信息）、物流、文化旅游等重点专业园区。有些特大型煤化工企业随着循环经济产业链的延伸已自我形成独立的经济园区。

5. 生态安全

秉承越是建设发展快，越要从严落实生态环保措施的理念，健全统筹发展机制。加强草原生态保护建设，实施禁牧、休牧和划区轮牧政策；加大沙地沙漠和水土流失治理力度，建设重点生态工程；加强环境保护和综合整治，大力推进节水节能减排，淘汰落后产能，发展循环经济，规范资源开发秩序。

Ordos city (former name is Ih Ju League) locates in the southwest of Inner Mongolia Autonomous Region, with a total population of 1.96 million in 2012; urbanization rate in this city reaches 72%. Total field in Ordos is about 86.700km^2, and there are a plenty of resources under and on this ground, 70% underground reserves coal which named Ordos as "Underground sea of coal".

One. Urban System Planning

According to "Ordos Urban System planning", this city shares an organic linked and rational divided development pattern by depart this whole place into a center city, two deputy central cities, 10 key town, 34 general towns (township, village) and 18 key industrial parks. Urban shares a high ability to gather population and elements support the social economy and affect the entire space in this city. Total population of Ordos in 2015 will be about 2.4 million with an 80% urbanization rate; the number will be 3.2 million and 93% in 2030.

Space structure: One primary, two deputies, four axes

One primary: refers to the primary center city consist of three places—Dongsheng, Kangbashi, Azhen. It is not only a producing base of energy, chemic, Cashmere clothing, IT and machinery manufacturing, but also a politic, economic, cultural and traffic center of Ordos.

Two deputies: means two deputy center cities—Xuejia Bay and Shulin League, which connected with two gateway cities—Hohhot and Baotou respectively.

Four axes: includes two development axes across in the center town and two axes surrounding the northern and southern of this city.

① Baoxi development axis: this axis relies on the towns and industrial areas distributes along the Baotou-Xi'an railway, expressway and National Highway 210 through the north to south. Its north connects with the urban agglomeration along the Yellow River and reaches to Mongol, while its south goes to Shanxi province directly and expands to southern cities. Towns including Shulin League, Ejinhoro, Zhasake and Ulanmulun are linked by this axis. ② Rong Wu development axis: this is an axis rely on Rongcheng-- Wuhai east-west expressway, National Highway 109, Dongwu Railway, and linked towns and cities like Checkerboards jing, Aolezhaoqi, Seney, Jungar Temple and Nuanshui. ③ Development axis along the Yellow River: supported by Beijing-Baotou-Lanzhou comprehensive transportation corridor and Freeway along the river, and plan to build industrial areas in Mengxi in Otog banner, DuGuiTaLa town in Hanggin Banner and Jungar Banner Road. ④ Development axis along the border: supported by Southern trunk way, it aims at building industrial areas and central towns in places including Shanghai Temple in Otog Front Banner, Tuke in Uxin Banner and Ulanmulun in Ejinhoro, connecting relevant cities like Shanxi and Ningxia.

Thus, it is much better to carry out systemic planning in key villages when speeding up the construction of urban areas, in this way to promote coordinated development of urban and rural areas.

Two. Regional Cooperation

Ordos occupies an important position in regional, provincial, even national development structure, by considering natural resources, geographic conditions, and economic conditions.

Ordos is the Growth Pole of Ordos–Baotou–Hohehot and cities along The Yellow River. It stands on the other side of Yellow River and waving to cities like Huhhot, Baotou, Bayannur, Wuhai City and Alxa League, which are now being combined into a whole by series of transport interface, and thus realizing the coordinated development with complementary advantages between different related cities.

Ordos is a core district of national Economic area of China north—central economic zone. Especially, the unique advantage can not be found in any other places that resource, industries and transportation network are overlapped with each others finely. Eight airports expect Erenhot Airport in this planning area are all located around Ordos, most towns can reach to at least one airport in less then 100km. What is more, this planning area connects with Yinchuan on the west and goes straight to Lanzhou; on its south is Yinlin and Yan'an—Xi'an Cluster, all these are helpful to build a diversified and all-round economic connection.

It is also a key wing of Beijing-Tianjin-Hebei metropolitan region and wreath Bohai Sea metropolis city cluster. Ordos Airport has an air distance of 500 km with Capital airport, while East Ordos is 600 km to Tianjin, highway and railway in Qinhuangdao Port. Also, it shares superior locational conditions on products exporting, information exchanging, traveling and importing.

Three. Transportation Network

Regional comprehensive transportation system is built based on the trunk highways and local railways, leading by regional key airports with inter-city railway, trunk railway lines and highways as the backbone. There are more and more flight course being built in Ordos, even through there have already been flights to many cities in China, in that case, more commuter airport are needed. Enhancing the capacity of railway transportation while strengthening this communications with the peripheral railway, thus a Huhhot-Baotou-Ordos interurban railway and a railway net with three horizontal and four lengthwise are formed. Highways in Ordos formed a # shaped highway net, by building a intensive transport net with eight horizontal and twelve lengthwise across eleven provincial extrance and twenty-seven bridges on Yellow River.

Four. The Fusion of urban and industry.

Focused on the key and deputy cities and four development axes, all kinds of industrial parks are being planed scientifically, which contacts comprehensive industrial parks as well as key professional industrial parks focus on mechanic, material, manufacturing, IT, logistics, culture and tourism. Some large Coal chemical enterprises have already changed into a self-independent economic area with the development extension of industrial chain of circular economy.

Five. Ecological Security

Ordos build a sound urban development mechanism, by upholding an idea that Ecological and environmental protection measures must follow the pace of constructive development. Measures are taken as followed: Strengthening grassland ecological protection and construction, implement the grazing, grazing and rotational grazing; straightening the controlling on sandy land and soil erosion, constructing key ecological projects. It is also important to enhance the environmental protection and comprehensive renovation when promoting water saving, energy conservation and emissions reduction. Closing down outdated production facilities, and developing a circle economy, thus resources can be exploited orderly.

一、城镇体系规划
City Planning

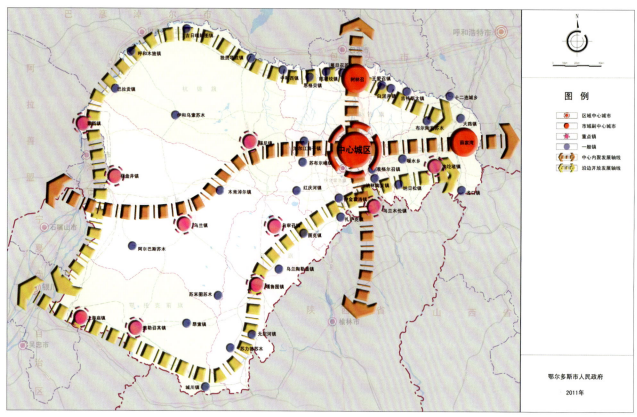

鄂尔多斯市空间结构规划（2011-2030）
Comprehensive Planning of Ordos City（2011-2030）

鄂尔多斯市域空间结构

2003年首次编制城镇体系规划，2010年进行修编。市域城镇空间结构为："一主两副四轴"。

"一主"是指中心城区。

"两副"是指树林召和薛家湾两个副中心城市。

"四轴"是指包西发展轴、荣乌发展轴、沿黄发展轴、沿边发展轴。

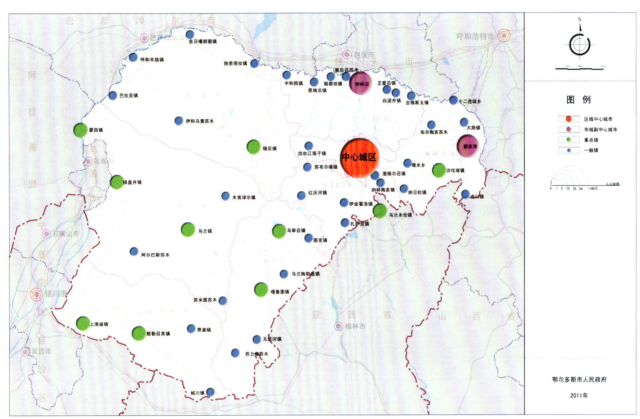

鄂尔多斯市城镇等级结构规划（2011–2030）
Comprehensive Planning of Ordos City（2011–2030）

鄂尔多斯市域城镇等级结构

　　区域中心城市与包头、呼和浩特市形成三角呼应的格局。
　　市域副中心城市：树林召、薛家湾两个副中心城市，与包头、呼和浩特市隔河呼应，发展成为以产业为主的综合型区域中心。
　　重点镇：包括旗府及重点产业园区所在镇。
　　一般镇：其他建制镇、苏木。

Urban Agglomeration in Ordos | 63

鄂尔多斯市中心城区
central urban area of Ordos City

21世纪初的东胜大广场 The Dongsheng square in the begining of 21 century

发展中的东胜 Dongsheng City

康巴什局部 Partial site of Kangbashi

阿镇局部 Partial site of Azhen

准格尔旗城市面貌
Urban landscape of Jungar Banner

准格尔旗薛家湾镇城市总体规划（2012–2030）
Overall planning for Jiawan County in Jungar Banner (2012–2030)

薛家湾一角　A corner of Xuejiawan Town

薛家湾塔哈拉川　Tajara River in Xuejiawan Town

薛家湾城市景观　Xuejiawan Town landscape

达拉特广场 Dalad square

达拉特旗城市面貌
Urban feature in Dalad Banner

达拉特城市总体规划（2008-2020）
Overall planning for Dalad Banner(2008-2020)

达拉特旗树林召镇鸟瞰
bird's eye view of Shulinzhao town in Dalad Banner

Urban Agglomeration in Ordos | 69

鄂托克旗城市面貌
Urban feature in Otog Banner

乌兰镇城市总体规划（2007-2020）
Overall planning for Ulan town in Otog Banner (2007-2020)

乌兰镇街景
Street scene in Ulan Town

乌兰广场一角
A corner of Ulan square

乌兰镇鸟瞰 Bird's eye view of Ulan Town

杭锦旗城市面貌
Urban feature in Hanggin Banner

杭锦旗锡尼镇城市总体规划（2010–2030）
Overall planning for Cenaea Town in Hanggin Banner (2010–2030)

锡尼镇街景
Street scene of Cenaea Town

锡尼镇生态居住区　Ecological Residential Community in Cenaea Town

乌审旗城市面貌
Urban feature in Uxin Banner

嘎鲁图镇鸟瞰 Aerial view of Galutu town

乌审旗嘎鲁图镇城市总体规划（2011–2030）
Overall planning for Galutu town in Uxin Banner (2011–2030)

嘎鲁图镇夜景 Night scene in Galutu town

嘎鲁图镇街景 Street scene of Galutu town

乌兰木伦河滨的康巴什新城
New Kangbashi city beside the UlanMulun River

康巴什夜景
Night view of Kangbashi

鄂托克前旗城市面貌
Urban feature in Otog Front Banner

敖勒召其镇全景 Panoramic view of Aolezhaoqi town

鄂托克前旗敖勒召其镇城市总体规划（2011–2030）
Overall planning for Aolezhaoqi town in Otog Front Banner (2011–2030)

街景 Street scene

敖勒召其镇出入口广场 Entrance Plaza view in Aolezhaoqi town

街景 Street scene

成吉思汗陵所在地——伊金霍洛镇
Ejinhoro town—where Genghis Khan mausoleum located

草原新城远眺 Overlooking the new-built City on Prairie

住宅小区 Residential area

蒙古特色建筑 Mongolian featured building

商业街 Commercial Street

伊金霍洛镇全景 Panoramic view of Ejinhoro town

二、区域合作
Regional cooperation

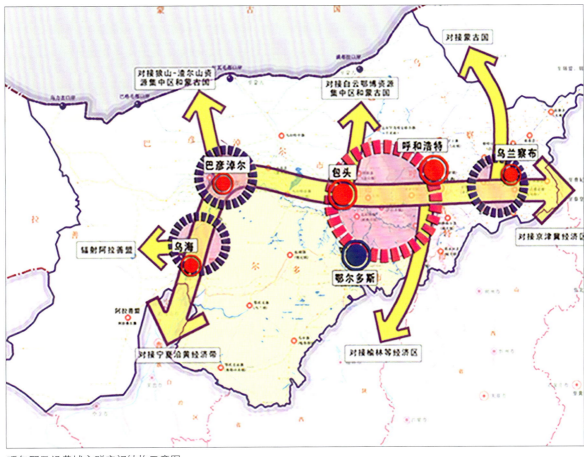

呼包鄂及沿黄城市群空间结构示意图
Spatial structure schematic diagram of city group including Baotou, Ordos and Hohhot

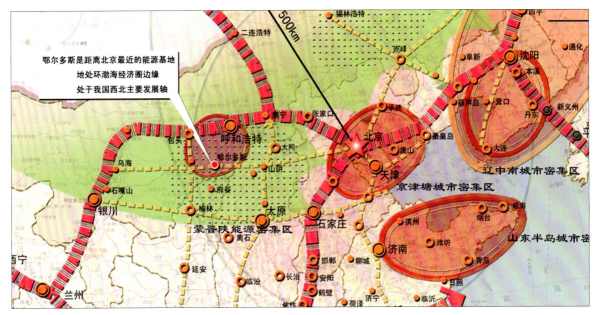

鄂尔多斯市与环渤海经济圈
Ordos city and the Bohai economic circle

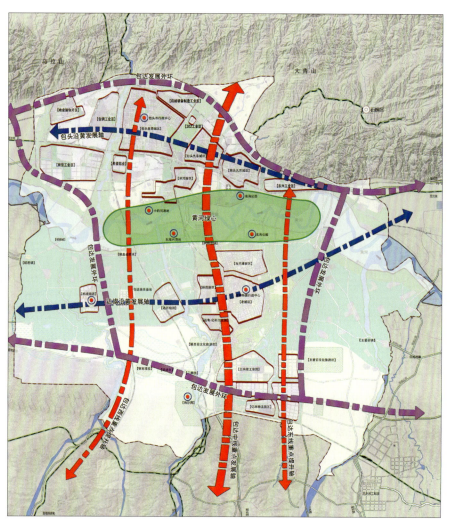

达拉特旗与包头市同城化规划图
City melt planning in Dalate and Baotou City

大路区与呼和浩特市协调发展图
Main roads and harmonious development graph in Hohhot

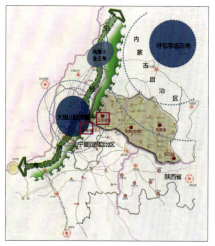

上海庙镇与宁东协调规划图
Coordinated planning graph between Shanghai Temple town and Ningdong town

三、城乡统筹、以城带乡
urban integrates with rural, rural steps after urban

对现有行政村分为城镇化村庄、重点发展村庄、基地型村庄、保留型村庄与迁移型村庄。

鄂尔多斯市城乡统筹规划（2011-2030）
Urban-rural coordinated plan in planning area in Ordos (2011-2030)

生态移民以城市带动为纽带
Ecological migration aiming at driving urban development

杭锦旗独贵塔拉镇住宅区 Residential area in DuGuiTaLa town in Hanggin Banner

杭锦旗移民小区 Immigrant community, Hanggin Banner

鄂托克前旗移民小区 Immigrant community, Otog Front Banner

鄂托克旗移民小区 Immigrant community, Otog Banner

梁家圪堵新农村 Liang Jia Ge Du New village

第三章

中心城区形态与布局

Chapter Three

Center City Layout and Form

鄂尔多斯——这一被世人所瞩目的高原明珠城市，经过世纪之交以来十多年的超常规发展，正在成为人们宜居、宜业、宜游、宜学的理想之地，也为后发展地区和资源富集地区加快城镇化进程提供了丰富经验。

1. 中心城区的由来与扩展

中华人民共和国成立之初，伊克昭盟行政公署设在原东胜县城。追溯近代历史，东胜于1907年设厅，1912年置县，1931年筑城，1984年变为县级市，2001年"撤盟设市"后成为鄂尔多斯市的中心城区。当时的建成区不足20平方公里，显然与全市经济社会发展和城镇化的龙头地位极不相称。进入21世纪以来，为了适应日新月异的发展形势，中心城区总体规划历经三次法定程序的编制和修编。

单中心规划——2000年版的规划提出，东胜城区应跨越包神铁路向西拓展，规划目标35万人、42平方公里。

双中心规划——面对城市预期规模迅速突破，原有城区受地形起伏、水资源匮乏、压覆矿产资源等多种因素制约，2004年版总体规划提出：中心城区应跳出东胜向南约20公里，在立地条件较好的康巴什建设新区，并和隔乌兰木伦河相连的伊金霍洛旗城关镇协调发展，形成"一城两区三个组团"（即：东胜—康巴什—阿镇）的格局，确定到2020年发展规模为65万人、68平方公里。中心城区多组团布局、路网连接、绿带相隔、舒展大气的生态城市格局初步形成。

带状城区规划——2010年城市实有人口达到80万，第二次规划的规模又提前突破。重新修编的新版总体规划立足于"三城区并行，产业园区拓展"的思路，积极推进康巴什与阿镇一体化建设并适当东拓、主要向北发展；东胜片区北控东收西优，主要向南拓展，形成南北相向对接发展的态势。

从"单中心"到"双核"跳跃式发展，再到"带状"相向对接式引导，每一次都不仅从"量"上实现了突破，也经历了"质"的提升。

2. 发展定位

根据现行总体规划，鄂尔多斯是国家重要的综合能源基地和新型化工基地，内蒙古自治区重要的经济增长极，富有民族文化特色的生态宜居城市。与此同时，更要建成区域性科技研发、人才培训、经济社会服务中心，以及蒙陕晋宁邻近地区的综合性交通运输枢纽。中心城区是鄂尔多斯市的政治、经济、文化中心。主要以汽车及工程装备制造、羊绒服装、信息工程、生物医药、金融贸易、总部经济、商贸物流、文化旅游等高端产业为主，形成规模化、集群化发展的经济园区。

3. 建设路径

近10多年来，依据总体规划的三次跨越式发展布局，始终坚持"先规划、后建设，先地下、后地上"的原则，围绕建设"国家园林城市"、"森林城市"、"生态环保城市"和"国际健康城市"的目标，努力破解原有"小城镇、大工业"的结构性矛盾。

新区建设。康巴什新城、东胜铁西新区、阿镇乌兰木伦新区等新建城区全部做到总体设计、分片控制、重点突出，节约资源、集约发展。基础设施、生态环境、社会服务、民生宜居等各类指标均瞄准国内、国际的一流水平。

棚户区改造。东胜与阿镇旧城改造还绿、还宜居、还健康于民。拆迁一片，建设一片，功能完善一片，由内到外分期分批推进。现已完成改造总量的70%以上。

经济产业支撑。中心城区用地规划安排足够的工业、商贸建设用地。大型产业经济园区在城区间和快速通道两侧合理布局。装备制造、云计算、空港物流等园区现已初具规模。

城乡统筹。罕台、铜川、万利、伊金霍洛等周边城镇贯彻总体规划意图，以绒纺、汽车博览、传统工艺、影视文化、体育运动及祭祀文化产业等为主进行组团式发展，转移安置农牧民，初步建成新型卫星新镇。

文化旅游扩展。东胜区建成"三园三川"（即：动物园、植物园、游乐园、三台基、罕台、吉劳庆川）和九城宫休闲旅游区、秦直道旅游文化园及各类文博馆。康阿片区建成乌兰木伦河旅游景区、亚洲雕塑艺术园、婚庆文化园、民族团结主题园、千亭山景区、F2赛车体育运动园、康巴什生态园、影视文化体育产业园、红海子湿地风景区和成吉思汗陵园风景区等著名文化园区，形成民族地域文化特色鲜明的生态旅游城市。其中，康巴什新区是全国第一个以城市命名的4A级旅游景区。此外新型产业、超大型企业也是特色旅游观摩的新领域。

4. 景观特色

鄂尔多斯的城市景观可以概括为：城外有林地环绕、街区有园林相间、道路有绿带相伴、建筑群疏密有致林草簇拥。城区建筑以浅淡清新的色系为主调，棕红、姜黄与白色相间。整个城市以舒展、大气、绿色、通透的视觉效果为建设主线，在现代风格中融入青铜文化、蒙元文化、自然生态等地域特色。

鄂尔多斯城市风貌的鲜明特色是生态园林城市的肌理十分明显。倘若从中心城区的最北端东胜区北郊出发，向南经康巴什到阿镇南端，城区内呈现出300米可见绿地、500米可见公园的格局；城区间无论走哪一条通道，都有绿带相随，林木相拥。随着绿地面积不断向城郊扩大，林草覆盖度不断提高，高原生态园林宜居城市的特色效果还在不断增强。

5. "舒展型"城市的条件和优势

鄂尔多斯能够形成"舒展型"城市形态，首先是缘于城市建设用地大都利用荒滩和沙地，较少受保护耕地"红线"的限制；其次是坚持注重绿地建设的方针，使城市建设变为区域生态环境建设的组成部分；再次是坚持科学规划，合理布局，均衡发展；还有就是抓住经济高速发展的机遇，打破建设资金不足的"瓶颈"。舒展型生态城市已经在根治交通拥堵、环境污染、生态恶化、服务不足、治安不良等各种"城市病"方面显现出巨大作用。与国内大多数"紧缩型"城市相比，鄂尔多斯几乎不存在交通阻塞和空气污染问题；与国外通常见到的"蔓延型"城市相比，鄂尔多斯不存在公共设施和服务难以覆盖的问题；与国际上推崇的"花园型"城市如堪培拉、巴西的巴西利亚、印度的昌迪加尔等相比，鄂尔多斯园林绿地并不少，而人气却要旺得多；与规划有效控制的世界名城华盛顿、莫斯科等相比，鄂尔多斯发扬了它们园林和建筑呈组团式相嵌的优点，同时经济产业布局还要胜出一筹。

Ordos, a plateau Pearl City attracted worldwide attention, is now an ideal place for living, learning, touring and undertaking after extraordinary development in these decades since the turn of the century. It also offers rich experiences for speeding up the urbanization in areas developed slowly and with rich resources.

One. Origin and Extension of Central City

Administrative office of Ikechosau League was set in former Donsheng County at the beginning of the establishment of the people's republic of China. Back into modern history, Dongsheng set up office in 1907 and set up county in 1912; in 1931, Dongsheng built fortification and changed into county-level city in 1984; finally, into a central city of Ordos in 2001 after the program "league to city". Built-up area was less then 20km^2 at that time, apparently disproportionate to the position of being the leader of economic and social development and urbanization in this whole city. To adapt to the rapid development of the situation, the general planning of central city got through three times of preparation and revision of legal procedures since the beginning of 21st century.

Single center planning—planning in 2000 which put forward that Dongsheng should expand to west across the Baotou-Shenmu Railway, with a scale of 350,000 citizens and 42km^2.

Double centers planning—due to the restrictions caused by topography, water scarcity and overlaid mineral resources, General planning in 2004 propose a new plan: central city should expand 20m^2 on the south of Dongsheng and set a new district in Kangbashi since site conditions were better there, then built a coordinated development relation with Chengguan Town in Ejinhoro Banner which connected by Ulanmulun River. Thus forming a group of one city two district (which is Dongsheng-Kangbashi-Azhen), predicted population would be 650.000 citizen in 68 km^2. The atmospheric and stretchy ecological urban structure was then initially formed with multi-group, connected highways and separated landscapes greenings.

Linear urban area planning—second planning was completed advanced since there were already 800,000 citizens in 2010. A new general planning was prepared based on the thought of expanding industrial park when paralleling three urban areas, to promote union construction between Kangbashi and Azhen as well as wertern and eastern development. Dongsheng District charges the development in north and collapsed in eastern development while optimizing the development of the west, and mainly develops toward south, thus forming a transfer situation with Kangbashi in the south.

Grown by leaps and bounds from "single-center" to "dual core", and to linear docking guidance, each planning achieved not only the breakthrough on quantity, but also on quality.

Two. Development Orientation

According to Current master plan, Ordos is not only a national key base of integrated energy and new chemical industry as well as a vital economic growing pole of Inner Mongolia Autonomous Region, but also a livable city with Ethnic and cultural characteristics. Meanwhile, it is also ready to be a regional center of R&D, personnel training and economic and social services, and a comprehensive transportation junction next to Inner Mongolia, shaanxi, Shanxi, Ningxia. Central city is the center of politics, economy and culture in Ordos. Main industries in this area includes automotive and engineering equipment manufacturing, cashmere clothing, IT, biomedicine, finance and trade, business logistics and cultural tourism; these high-end industries form a scale and clustered developing economic park.

Three. Path construction

In the past 10 years, according to three development plans for general planning, this area insist a principle that "plan before construction, underground before up ground", with the goal to build a national gardening, foresting, eco-friendly and international sound city, by trying to solve the structural contradictions of "small town, large industry".

Construction of new district: new built metropolitan areas including Kangbashi, Tiexi New District in Dongsheng and Ulanmulun in Azhen all stress on overall plan with clear area decomposition and outstanding key point, as well as saving resources to develop intensively. Each kind of index of infrastructure, environment, social services and livelihood are all regulated by first-class regulation in China, and even in the world.

Shantytown renovation: Dongsheng and Azhen dedicate to change the old cities into green, sound and livable new places. Once an area is removed, it would be completed on functions and facilities by progress gradually from different stages. There are more than 70% of the total renovation have been finished.

Economic and industrial support: there are enough land have been arranged for industrial and business uses in the land plan of central city. With large industrial and economic park distributed properly on the sides of expressways and between cities, parks for manufacturing, cloud computing and airport logistics now begin to take shape.

Urban-rural Integration: Hantai, Tongchuan, Wanli, Ejinhoro and other surrounding towns all implement the purpose of layout plan, and develop by uniting Cashmere spinning, Auto Expo, Traditional crafts, Television Culture, Sports, Ritual culture and other industries, meanwhile, transfer and settle Farmers and herdsmen; and thus build new satellite town step by step.

Cultural tourism expansion: Dongsheng district has constructed "three parks and three gullies" (which means zoo, botanical garden, amusement park, Sanjitai, Hantai and Jilaoqing Gully) and Jiucheng Palace leisure tourism area, Qin straight-way Tourist Culture Garden and all kinds of cultural museum. In Kangbashi-Azhen district, Eco tourism city with unique ethnic and local culture features has been formed due to the famous cultural parks like Asian Sculpture Art Park, Wedding Culture Park, Ethnic Unity Park, Qianding Mount spot, F2 racing park, Kangbashi Ecological Park, Red Lake Wetland Park, Genghis Khan Mausoleum and so on. Kangbashi New District is the first 4A tourism attraction named after the city's name in our country. Beside, new type of industries and super enterprises are also new places to visit.

Four. Landscape Features

Landscape in Ordos can be described as this: forests cover the outside, gardens separate the blocks while greenbelt following along the roads and grasses spreading around the buildings. Colors of buildings in central city are mainly slight and fresh, such as reddish brown and turmeric combined with white. This whole city make the comfortable, green, expanding and transparent vision efforts into a main tone, and blending bronze culture, Yuan Culture, natural ecology and local characters into modern style.

A distinctive characteristic of Ordos is the apparent skin texture of ecological garden city. If you start at the north of Dongsheng in the north of central city, go straight toward south through Kangbashi to south of Azhen, you can finely see the garden in every 300m and park in every 500m. Wherever you go, greenbelt and tall trees follows along. Meanwhile, vegetation coverage is now adding because of the growing green areas, as a result, the feature character of being a ecological and livable city is strengthening.

Five. Conditions and Advantages of Stretch-type city

First reason for Ordos to be a stretch-type city is the land used for urban construction is mainly desert and wasteland which are less limited by the protection of arable land. Second is that the area stress on Greenland construction, which makes urban construction into an important part of regional ecological environment. The third reason is the scientific plan, proper layout and balanced development. Last but not the least, a chance to speed up the economic development, which helps greatly to solve funds needed in construction. Stretched ecologic city makes great efforts in bringing under permanent control on all kinds of "urban disease" like traffic congestion, environmental pollution, ecological deterioration, inadequate service and disorder, etc. Compared with most domestic "crunch type" city, Ordos is barely suffered from the traffic jam and air pollution, while it has no problem on public facilities and services when comparing with "Spread-type" City out of China. What is more, Ordos has a equal green land coverage with the international Gardening cities such as Canberra, Brasilia, Chandigarh, but enjoys a much better popularity. Also, when speaks to world famous cities with effective control of city planning including Washington and Moscow, Ordos wins a chip on the economic and industrial layout while carry forward the advantages of combining of gardens and buildings.

一、城市扩展
urban sprawl

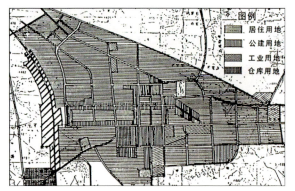

东胜市城市总体规划（1992-2010）
Master Plan in Dongsheng (1992-2010)

东胜规划人口 20 万,是伊克昭盟的政治、经济和文化中心。

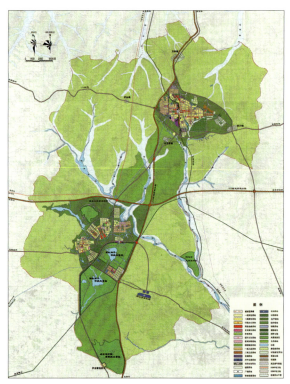

鄂尔多斯市城市总体规划（2004-2020）
Master Plan in Ordos (2004-2020)

形成总人口达到 65 万人,城市建设用地控制在 68 平方公里,和"一城两区、三组团"的空间布局。

乌审街 Uxin Street

鄂尔多斯街 Ordos street

铁东商圈 Tiedong business circle

伊金霍洛街街景 Scene of Ejinhoro street

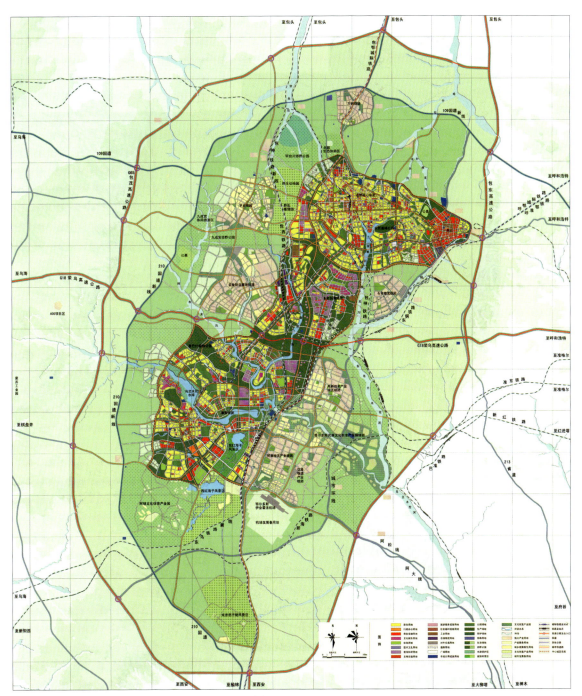

鄂尔多斯市城市总体规划（2011-2030）- 用地规划
Master Plan in Ordos(2011-2030)—land-use planning

　　新版城市总体规划2030年人口达到240万人，城市建设用地为325平方公里，城市远景整体向西发展。

Center City Layout and Form

二、道路交通系统
Road Traffic System

　　城市中心区路网整体呈环状结构,道路结构划分为快速路、主干路、次干路、支路四个等级,其中快速路为"十一横六纵"。

中心城区道路交通系统规划(2011-2030)
Traffic system planning in central urban area (2011-2030)

装备制造基地立交　Well-equipped to build base Overpass

东胜西立交　Lesheng west Overpass

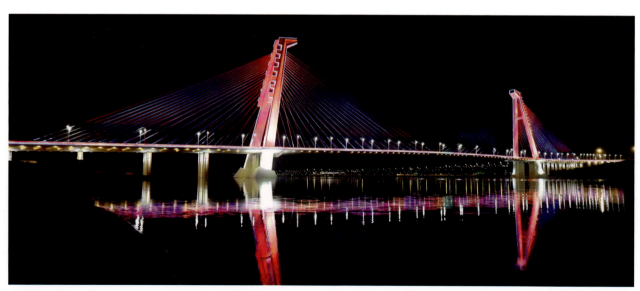

跨乌兰木伦河4号桥　No.4 Bridge cross the Ulanmulun River

包神铁路 Baotou-Shenmu railway

东康快速路 Dong Kang Expressway

康巴什鄂尔多斯大街 Kangbashi Ordos Street

三、市区主导产业拮英
Leading Industry Confluence

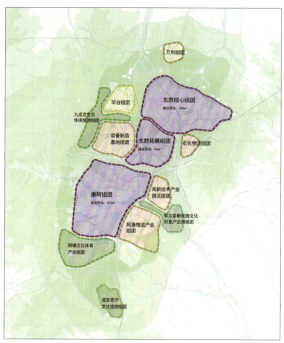

中心城区组团分析（2011-2030）
Analysis on cluster in central area (2011-2030)

羊绒产业中心 Cashmere industry center

太阳能光伏电池板生产线 Solar photovoltaic panels production line

铜川汽车博览园 Tongchuan Auto Expo Park

汽车生产线 Automobile production line

四、城市面貌
Urban feature

东胜城市一角 A corner of Dongsheng City

棚户区改造后的新貌 New appearance of squatter after transformation

东胜城区南界面局部 Dongsheng City Southern Local Interface

康巴什新区
Kangbashi new area

康巴什中心轴（北向）Central shaft of Kangbashi (north orientation)

康巴什中心轴（南向）Central shaft of Kangbashi (south orientation)

Center City Layout and Form | 105

康巴什夜景
Night view in Kangbashi

康巴什局部夜景 Night view in Partial Kangbashi

康巴什中心轴夜景 Night view in central shaft of Kangbashi

Center City Layout and Form

乌兰木伦河两岸风光
Scenery on both sides of Ulanmulun River

北岸为康巴什新区 Kangbashi new area on the north side

南岸为阿镇新区 Azhen new area on the south side

Center City Layout and Form | 109

阿镇城市面貌
appearance of Azhen

阿镇城景 Landscape of Azhen

阿镇城市局部 Partial site of Azhen

阿镇夜景 Night view in Azhen

主干道街景
Main expressway

鄂尔多斯大街
Ordos street

康巴什——鄂尔多斯大街 Ordos street, Kangbashi

东胜——达拉特南路 South Dalad Road, Dongsheng

114 中心城区形态与布局

东胜——万正路 Wanzheng Road, Dongsheng

阿镇——通格朗路 Tonggelang Road, Azhen

康巴什——团结街 Unity Street, Kangbashi

康巴什——正阳街 Zhengyang Street, Kangbashi

东胜一角 A corner of Dongsheng

东胜——伊金霍洛街 Ejinhoro Street, Dongsheng

康巴什——呼和塔拉路 Hohtara Road, Kangbashi

东胜——鄂尔多斯东街 East Ordos Street, Dongsheng

东胜——鄂尔多斯西街 West Ordos Street, Dongsheng

东胜——天骄路 Tianjiao Road, Dongsheng

Center City Layout and Form | 117

五、城市功能拮英
Confluence of Urban Functions

北京师范大学 – 鄂尔多斯附属学校
Beijing Normal University Ordos Affiliated School

鸟瞰图 Airscape

鄂尔多斯市第一中学
The First Middle School of Ordos City

校园东门 East Gate of Campus

校园北门 North Gate of Campus

校园全景 Campus's panorama

中心广场 Center Plaza

Center City Layout and Form | 121

康巴什蒙古族幼儿园
Kangba Mongolian Kindergarten

康巴什新区第一小学
The first primary school in Kangbashi New District

鄂尔多斯市蒙古族学校
Ordos Mongolian school

鸟瞰图 Airscape

南门 South Gate

鄂尔多斯那达慕运动场
Nadam sports field of Ordos city

鄂尔多斯那达慕运动场位于伊金霍洛旗阿镇，于 2009 年开工建设。总占地面积 83 公顷，总建筑面积 75000 平方米。本工程设计功能为民族体育综合性运动和训练场，主要包括办公区、运动场、看台区、赛马场、停车场、水系、硬绿化、道路、中心广场以及其他附属配套设施等。那达慕运动场由北京市建筑设计研究院设计。

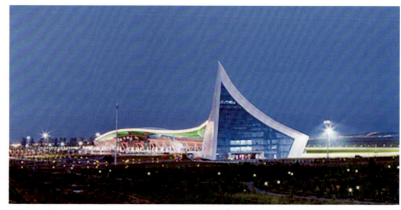
夜景 Night

全景 Panoramic

正面 Facade

鄂尔多斯金港湾 F2 国际赛车场
Ordos Golden Harbor F2 International Autodrome

鄂尔多斯国际赛车场是拥有国际二级赛道的大型国际赛车场。

赛道全长 3.751 公里，路面宽度 12～15 米，最大落差 32 米，被称为中国第一条国际山地赛道。共 18 个弯道，设计最高时速达 296 公里/小时。赛道形如驰骋的骏马，主看台形如展翅飞翔的雄鹰，显示了鄂尔多斯浓郁的地域文化。

平面图 Plan

赛车场正面 Frontispiece of Autodrome

比赛场景 Racing scene

曲折跑道 Winding Track

选手入场 Racer entering Autodrome

Center City Layout and Form | 127

鄂尔多斯市中心医院
Ordos Central Hospital

正门 Front door

住院部 Inpatient Department

休闲广场 Leisure Square

鄂尔多斯蒙医医院
Ordos Mongolian Hospital

王府路社区卫生服务站
Wangfu Road Community health service stations

城市商业中心
City Commercial Center

每天百货都市 Everyday Department Store

王府井 Wangfujing

金辰国际购物中心 Jinchen International Shopping center

商业区 Commercial District

民生广场 Minsheng Square

万正广场 Wanzheng Square

国贸百货 Guomao Emporium

Center City Layout and Form | 131

康巴什美食广场
Kangbashi Food Square

Center City Layout and Form | 133

街道社区
Community

服务大厅 Service hall

党建工作展厅 Party Cconstruction Exhibition Hall

体育健身活动室 Fitness Gym

棋牌室 Chess Room

图书阅览室 Library reading room

电子阅览室 Digital Reading Room

休闲讲堂 Lecture Room

香茶室 Tearoom

伊金霍洛旗王府路社区
Wangfu Road community in Ejinhoro Banner

服务大厅 Service Hall

亲子乐园 Parent-child paradise

爱心室 Benevolence room

活动室 Activity room

伊泰华府住宅小区
Yitai Huafu residential community

康和丽舍住宅小区
Kanghe Lishe residential community

Center City Layout and Form

锦绣山庄住宅小区
Splendid Villa Residential community

Center City Layout and Form | 143

满世尚都住宅小区
Manshi Shangdu Residential Community

Center City Layout and Form

东方纽蓝地住宅小区
Oriental Newland residential community

康城住宅小区 1-4 期
Kangcheng residential 1-4 period

Center City Layout and Form | 149

城乡统筹示范园区
urban-rural integration Demonstration Park

鄂尔多斯文化活动
Cultural Activities in Ordos

第十一届亚洲艺术节闭幕式
The closing ceremony of 11th Asia Arts Festival

第一届国际那达慕大会比赛场景
Competing scene of 1st International Nadam Festival

第二届国际那达慕大会开幕式
Opening ceremony of 2nd International Nadam Festival

第三届国际草原文化节开幕式
Opening ceremony of 3rd International Prairie Culture Festival

第四章

园林广场

Chapter Four

Garden & Square

园林广场群是鄂尔多斯绿地生态建设成果和城市文化特色的集中展示。到 2012 年底,全市公园广场超过 200 个,其中位于中心城市的 75 个。人均公园绿地面积由 10 年前的 0.6 平方米增加到 29.05 平方米,城区绿化覆盖率达到 40% 以上。建筑群和园林广场交错、城市与园林绿带融为一体的风貌特色十分明显。

1. 生态园林

这类园林一般位于城市边缘,具有占地面积大、植物种类多、自然风貌浓郁、内部结构多样、生态效应强的特点。近年新建、改建的著名生态园林有东胜森林公园、东胜区的三园三川,康阿生态园、千亭山景区、红海子湿地风景区、成吉思汗陵园景区以及东康快速路两侧宽 300 米以上的带状园林。

2. 主题文化广场

这类广场本着控制硬化、增加绿化的精神进行建设,园中有林,林中有园,广场融入园林之中。广场主题一般表现地域文化特色。比较多的有成吉思汗英雄史诗类、自然历史类、蒙元文化类、重大事件纪念类等。在一般综合性园林的建设中也大量使用地域元素,如蒙古包、祥云、哈达、牧民生活、蒙古族服饰、鄂尔多斯婚礼、马头琴、辘辘车、奔马、苍狼、牛羊等草原风情。

在康巴什新区,主题文化生态广场群构成了城市的核心,这就是北起鄂尔多斯市党政大楼前的市政广场,南到乌兰木伦河北岸的东西宽约 200 米、南北长约 2600 米的中央景观绿带,由北往南依次可观赏到步移景异的成吉思汗广场、市民演艺广场、天驹广场、太阳广场、蒙古象棋广场、市民休闲广场、亚洲雕塑艺术主题公园、乌兰木伦湖中心广场。在康巴什与阿镇分界处,则有东西向的融水面、绿带、道路、壁画、石窟于一体的滨河景观带。

在东胜区,无论是新建城区还是原有城区,随处可见城景相融、视觉通透的生态休闲空间。这与 10 多年前居民只有到两三个拥挤不堪的狭小广场才能进行户外活动形成明显反差。以东胜公园为节点,东西方向可见站前广场、商务休闲广场等景观带,由北往南可见山体公园、市政广场、青铜文化广场等景观带。两带交叉形成宽度为 60—380 米向四面呈带状延伸、文化与生态交融的广场集群。这些综合性景观通廊的建设进一步完善了城市功能,优化了整体服务环境,使城市品位显著提高。

3. 市民休闲广场

散布于全城、建于居住区附近的休闲广场除了文化、生态功能外，增设了供居民游乐、健身的各种设施，成为居民户外活动、联谊交往的重要场所。广场中开阔的绿地、水面、树林，也是市民应急避险的备用场所。现在居住在鄂尔多斯，广场活动已经成为日常生活的重要组成部分。这类广场在东胜区有扩建后的伊克昭广场、站前广场、林荫广场、怡景苑广场、亿利华庭广场、人民公园、假日公园等；在康巴什有玫瑰广场、会展广场、草原情广场、视界广场、婚庆公园、仁和园等多处休闲场所。在休闲广场通常每天都汇集成百成千的市民，对丰富文化生活、增进身心健康、提高幸福指数、促进社会和谐具有不可或缺的作用。

4. 建筑组团分隔绿带

以绿带隔离建筑群、控制建筑密度是营造舒展型和生态型城市风貌的重要途径。例如，乌兰木伦河两岸300—500米宽的滨河绿化带，乔木灌木与花卉草坪组合相嵌构成一幅幅美丽的画卷。茂盛的绿化带与城市建筑相间，改善了城市的生态环境和人居环境，实现了人与自然和谐共处。然而，这一绿带最独特的作用是把康巴什和阿镇两大城区永久性地分割开来，整个城市结构形成河水穿城流过、两岸绿带和滨河大道并行、建筑群疏密相间的独特景观。这在中西部城市十分罕见。

5. 多种形式的社会园林

除政府投资大量兴建公共园林外，鼓励全社会广泛开展园林式机关、园林式住宅区、园林式企业的建设。近年还出现了室内园林和园林式矿区等增绿形式。

鄂尔多斯在城市建设中能够大规模营造林草绿地，除了利用沙地、沟壑等非农用地的政策环境外，积极推进乡土植物的选优、培育与应用，能够取得成本低、见效快的效果也是重要条件。各地普遍优先使用沙地柏、油松、馒头柳、山桃、山杏、榆树、沙枣、黄刺玫、柠条等本土树种，充分发挥了适应性强、地方特色鲜明、易于管理的优势。引进的五十多个品种林木也要求兼顾抗旱耐寒能力强、观赏价值高等特点，以期尽快取得良好的绿化效果。

Garden and square are the showcase of ecologic constructing achievements and urban cultural features of Ordos. There are more then 200 gardens and squares in the whole city in the end of 2012, and 75 among those are in the central city. Per capita green area has added to 29.05㎡ instead of 0.6㎡ ten years ago, with a green coverage more then 40%. The landscape features which is a combination of building groups, gardens and squares, urban and greenbelts is extremely outstanding.

One. Ecologic Gardens

This kind of gardens is always located at the edge of cities with characters of large area, various plants, rich natural landscape, diverse internal structure and strong ecological effects. Famous ecologic built and rebuilt in recent years are Dongsheng Forest Park, "three parks and three gullies", Kangbashi-Azhen ecologic park, Qianting Mount Spot, Red Lake Wetland Park, Genghis Khan Mausoleum and linear parks all the way along the sides of Dong Kang Expressway for more then 300m.

Two. Thematic Cultural Square

These squares were constructed on the purpose of Control the hardening and increasing forestation, to make forest in parks, parks in forest and squares into gardens. Themes of squares are mainly local cultural features, so most of them are showing the heroes in Genghis Khan Period, natural history, Yuan and Mongolian cultures, memorable events, etc. there are also many local elements in the common comprehensive gardens, such as yurt, auspicious clouds, Hada, nomadic life, Mongolia nationality clothing, Ordos wedding, Mongol stringed instrument, horses, wolf, sheep and cattle.

In Kangbashi, thematic cultural squares are the core of this city. This is Municipal Square if front of Erdos Party and Government Office, with a central landscape about 200m wide and 2600m long next to the north bank of Ulanmulun River. Landscapes of Genghis Khan Square, People's Performing Square, Sun Plaza, Mongolia chess square、Asian Sculpture Art Park and other parks from the south to north along this way. Also, there are some Riverside Landscape Belts toward west which gathers water, greenbelt, roads, murals and caves, at the parting of Kangbashi and Azhen.

Ecological leisure space of urban landscape integration, visual permeability can be seen everywhere in Dongsheng, no matter in the new-built district or in the old district. This makes a great contrast with small squares in ten years ago which is crowd and not enough for outdoor living. Standing at Dongsheng park, we can see landscapes made by Front Plaza and leisure plaza to the west and east, while Municipal plaza, Bronze Culture Park on the north and south. These two landscapes on different directions form a cultural and ecologic square group with a width 60-380m, spreading around on four directions. The construction of these comprehensive landscapes further complete urban functions, optimize overall service environment and promote the city grade

Three. Public leisure Square

public leisure Squares built near the residential areas in the whole city not only function as cultural and ecologic sites, but also a important place for citizen to take outdoor activities and social intercourse by adding recreation, fitness facilities. Also, wide Greenland, waters and forests in the squares are good place to go in emergency. As a result of that, square activities have been a big part of daily life for people living in Ordos. This kind of square in Dongsheng includes reconstructed Ikechosau Park, Front Plaza, avenue plaza, Yili Square, People's park and Holiday Park, while leisure parks like Rose Square, Convention Square, Caoyuanqing Square, Horizon Park, Wedding Culture Park and Renhe Garden are in Kangbashi. There are thousands of people gathered in squares; that plays an indispensable role in enriching cultural life, strengthening healthy, improving happiness index and promoting social harmony.

Four. Building group & separation greenbelt

Using greenbelt to separate building groups and control building density is an important way to create stretch and ecologic city. Take the 300-500m Riverfront Green Belt beside Ulanmulun River as an example, trees, shrubs, lawns and flowers combines with each others and form beautiful pictures. Lush green belt alternate with urban buildings can improve eco-environment and living environment in city, and thus achieving a harmonious coexistence between man and nature. However, the most incredible function of this greenbelt is to split Kangbashi off Azhen permanently, in this way, structure of this city enjoys a special landscape that river flows in the center with greenbelt on both side, and building group keep a particular density. This can barely be seen in middle and western cities.

Five. Multi-formed Social Garden

A large number of governmental investments are used on public gardening, to encourage society to construct garden-style office, residential areas and business buildings. There are also some new greening forms in recent years, such as indoor gardens, garden-mining and so on.

The reason Ordos can built large scale of green lands during the construction in not only because of non-farm lands like the sandy lands and gullies; Ordos also promotes cultivation and application of local plants, which is a important way to achieve great effort with a low cost. sabina vulgaria, Chinese pine, Prunus davidiana, Elaeagnus angustifolia, caragana microphylla and other local trees are first choice to Give full play to the advantages including strong adaptability, distinctive local characteristics and easy to manage. More than 50 kinds of trees introduced from other places are also required to take drought resistant ability and ornamental value into account, in order to obtain good greening effect as soon as possible.

成吉思汗广场
Genghis Khan square

位于康巴什新区,建成于 2006 年。以地域特色为景观设计理念,分为三个主题:团结、乡情和生态自然。

全景 Panorama

Garden & Square | 163

蒙古象棋广场
Mongolia chess square

位于康巴什新区,面积约 5 公顷,通过绿化、地貌、人行与车行出入口建筑等来组织围合空间,象征走向现代文明的鄂尔多斯"开放包容、实现跨越"的精神。

全景 Panorama

棋子雕像局部 Part of Pawn statue

棋子雕像局部 Part of Pawn statue

Garden & Square | 165

亚洲雕塑艺术主题公园
Asian Sculpture Art Park

　　位于成吉思汗广场轴线的南端,乌兰木伦河北侧。公园总面积约41.9公顷,绿地率约70%,以鄂尔多斯青铜器原型的放大雕塑为主,汇集了亚洲部分国家的雕塑作品。

全景 Panorama

青铜器主雕 Main Carving– Bronze Vessels

Garden & Square

康巴什中心公园
Kangbashi centre Park

建于 2008 年，占地 27.54 公顷，以山坡为主，其中绿化面积约 20 公顷。设计突出生态，与科技会展中心相得益彰，打造高品质的城市中心开放性主题公园。

绿化景观 Greening landscape

视界公园
Horizon Park

位于鄂尔多斯会展中心南侧，面积约 14.9 公顷，规划以主题雕塑"视界"与会展中心遥相呼应寓意"慧眼看世界"的设计理念。

主题景观 Theme landscape

Garden & Square | 171

鄂尔多斯婚庆文化园
Ordos Wedding Culture Park

以展示鄂尔多斯蒙古族婚礼以及中国传统婚礼和爱情文化为主题的公园，占地约 43 公顷。

入口 Entrance

Garden & Square

草原情广场
Caoyuanqing Square

　　面积 15.98 万平方米，以"草原之歌"为设计主题展现了鄂尔多斯深厚的文化内涵，独特的自然风景，热情浓烈的人文和多彩的民族风情。

Garden & Square | 175

鄂尔多斯广场
Ordos square

全景 Panorama

绿化之初 Early stage of greening

晨练场景 Morning exercises

爱拥公园
Aiyong Park

全景 Panorama

图腾柱 Totem-pole

绿化效果 Greening

民族团结公园
Ethnic Unity Park

位于康巴什新区，面积约为222.4公顷，公园主要景观为56个民族的团结柱。

全景 Panorama

团结柱 Unity pole

掌岗图公园
Zhanggangtu Park

位于阿镇，占地面积230公顷。重点体现了蒙元文化、绿色生态，"以塞外风情、草原牧歌"为主题，形成滨水生活休闲带和"长河旭日"、"蒙元沧桑"、"深林探幽"和"城市港湾"等特色景观区。

伊克昭公园
Ikechosau Park

2007年将人民公园更名伊克昭主题公园以表达原伊克昭盟的城市轨迹。

Garden & Square | 181

青铜文化广场
Bronze Culture Park

位于东胜区，总占地面积 10 万平方米，广场绿化面积 5.8 万平方米，分为地上和地下两个部分，以"太阳"穹顶，"月亮"建筑及鄂尔多斯青铜群雕为肢体组成，主要功能为室内展厅，绿地广场和雕塑群。

全景 Panorama

Garden & Square | 183

东胜公园
Dongsheng Park

建于 2005 年 8 月，总占地面积为 23.86 万平方米，绿地面积 17 万平方米，水体面积 2.2 万平方米，一处利用自然地形地貌进行植物造景，水体为辅的下沉式公园，也是集娱乐、休闲、游览等多功能为一体的开放式公园。

全景 Panorama

局部 Section

局部 Section

音乐喷泉 Musical fountain

Garden & Square | 185

市政广场
Municipal plaza

建于 2005 年，总占地面积 101376 平方米。楼前广场、中心广场、东广场、西广场以及四周绿地五部分组成。

全景 Panorama

局部 Section

绿地 Landscape

花坛 Parterre

局部 Section

Garden & Square

假日公园
Holiday Park

假日公园位于东胜区，于 2007 年 8 月份全面完成建设，总占地面积 11.5 公顷。

祥云水上公园（三台基水库）
Xiangyun water park (Santaiji Reservoir)

位于东胜区，绿化面积131.1万平方米，水域面积135万平方米。该公园分为三台基库区滨水绿化带、滨湖公园区和滨河广场区。

火车站站前广场
Front Plaza of Train Station

建于 2003 年 10 月，总占地面积为 20242 平方米，绿地面积 7764 平方米。象征着东胜区经济繁荣，城市建设蒸蒸日上。

全景 Panorama

气象公园
Qixiang Park

位于东胜区，总占地 13.1 万平方米。

鹿苑广场
Luyuan Square

位于东胜区，总占地面积4.45万平方米，以大面积草坪景观为主，辅以旱地溪流景观，并用小喷泉加以点缀，景观与鹿群相互呼应。

三角洲公园
Delta Park

位于东胜区，总占地面积18.6公顷，绿化面积15.8公顷。

入口 Entrance

观景道 Scenery lane

局部 Section

小品 Statue

Garden & Square | 197

植物园
Botanical Garden

位于东胜区郊外

入口广场 Entrance square

Garden & Square | 199

植物园全景 Panorama of Botanical Garden

山桃 Prunus Davidiana Franch

杏 Apricot

旱柳 Salix matsudana

榆树 Elm

沙枣 Elaeagnus Angustifolia

红柳 Branchy tamarisk

Garden & Square | 201

动物园
Zoo

位于东胜区郊外

入口广场 Entrance Square

全景 Panorama

景观 Landscape

部分动物 Partial animals

Garden & Square

百鸟苑 Aviary

百鸟苑内景 Interior of Aviary

火烈鸟馆 Flamingo House

葵花鹦鹉 Cockatoo

火烈鸟 Flamingo

灰雁游荡 Swimming Grey Goose

母亲公园
Mother's Park

位于伊金霍洛旗阿镇,占地133公顷,建于2009年。取材于成吉思汗母亲的史迹,与成吉思汗陵处于同一轴线上,由山丘绿地、雕塑、文化廊等组成。

远眺母亲公园 Overlooking Mother's park

母亲公园雕塑及公园全景
Sculpture in Mother's park and panorama

局部 Section

人民广场
People's Square

位于阿镇,建于2005年,总面积11020平方米,绿地面积达4898平方米,水域面积达1650平方米,硬化面积4472平方米。

Garden & Square | 209

阿吉奈公园
Ajina Park

位于阿镇，总面积 18 公顷。以水系、水景为主体，以生态、休闲、娱乐、健身为主题。

公园入口 Ajina Park

柳河沟公园
The willow Brook Park

位于阿镇城市中心地段，建设于2009年。河道景观4.04千米，宽70-300米，总面积76公顷，绿地面积52.8公顷。以河中高差不同的景观瀑布和跌水形成的连接水面为线索，选择柳属植物树种，形成一带一园二节点的景观。

红海子湿地公园
Red Lake Wetland Park

  伊金霍洛旗东西红海子湿地公园位于阿镇,始建于2011年,占地面积3700公顷,依据蒙古民族气贯长虹的发展史,对东西红海子景观规划提出了"盛世华章"的整体理念,其中包含了历史、文化、生态、景观、发展等篇章。

Garden & Square | 215

中心城区街心公园
center street park of central urban area

哈达公园花瓣广场 Petals Square in Hada Park

东胜林荫广场 Dongsheng avenue plaza

阿镇小游园 Azhen small garden

东胜亿利文化广场 Dongsheng Yili Cultural plaza

Garden & Square | 217

达拉特旗白塔公园
Dalad Banner White Pagoda Park

位于树林召镇区中部，占地面积 47 公顷，依托古塔建园以体现文化底蕴。

入口花圃 Entrance flowerbeds

景观 Landscape

公园一角 A Corner of Park

鄂托克旗西鄂尔多斯文化主题公园
Otog Banner Ordos culture park

位于鄂托克旗乌兰镇,总占地面积约17公顷(其中赛马场占地7公顷,文化主题公园占地10公顷),具有时代特色和地域风情,满足市民休闲、娱乐、浏览需求。

局部 Section

水景 Waterscape

全景 Panorama

局部 Section

乌审旗鸿沁湖公园
Uxin Banner Hongqin Lake Park

位于嘎鲁图镇石化创业新区内。鸿沁湖公园东西全长1300米、南北宽500米,贯穿东西三个街区、南北两个区块,总占地面积25万平方米。

主题雕塑——取材于人居环境奖图案
The main sculpture

鄂托克前旗鹰骏公园
Otog Front Banner Eagle Park

全景 Panorama

局部 section

局部 section

Garden & Square | 225

杭锦旗锡尼广场
Hanggin Banner Seney Square

建于居住区中间,地域特色和休闲功能有机结合。

全景 Panorama

准格尔旗南山公园
Jungar Banner Nanshan Park

借助荒山绿化建成的生态公园。为薛家湾镇"山水城市"的景观组成部分。

Garden & Square | 229

二、乡土园林植物选录
Selected native garden plants

樟子松 Pinus sylvestris

白扦 Picea meyeri

新疆杨 Populus bolleana lauche

银白杨 White poplar

青海云杉 Picea crassifolia

旱柳 Salix matsudana

国槐 Sophora japonica

侧柏 Platycladus orientalis

杜松 Hackmatack

龙爪槐 Sophora japonica var

金叶榆 Ulmus pumila cv.jinye

白蜡 Fraxinus sogdiana Bunge

山桃 Prunus Davidiana Franch

丝绵木 Euonymus bungeanus Maxim

皂荚 Gleditsia sinensis Lam

山杏 Siberian Apricot

一串红 Salvia splendens　　　　　金盏菊 Calendula officinalis

小丽花 Dahlia pinnate　　　　　大丽花 Dahlia pinnate

万寿菊 Tagetes erecta　　　　　彩叶草 Coleus blumei Benth

美女樱 Verbena hybrida　　紫花苜蓿 Medicago sativa

孔雀草 Maidenhair　　蜀葵 Althaea rosea　　千屈菜 Lythrum salicaria

百日草 Zinnia elegans　　三色堇 Viola tricolor hortensis

Garden & Square | 235

丁香 Syringa oblata

连翘 Forsythia suspensa

榆叶梅 Amygdalus triloba

玫瑰 Rugosa rose

紫穗槐 Amorpha fruticosa

珍珠梅 Sorbaria kirilowii

叉子圆柏（沙地柏）
Juniperus Sabina (Sabina vulgaris)

红瑞木
Cornus alba

紫叶小檗
Berberisthunbergiicv.atropurpurea

小叶女贞 Ligustrum quihoui

柠条 Caragana Korshinskii Kom

沙柳 Salix

柽柳 Tamarix Chinensis

接骨木 Erberry

枸杞 Lyciun chinense Mill.

Garden & Square | 237

第五章 建筑风貌

Chapter Five

Architectural Features

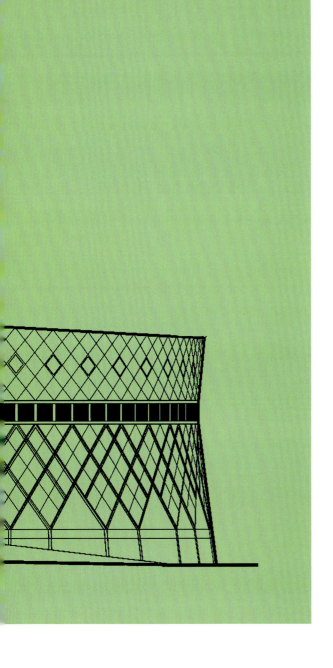

鄂尔多斯——这个地处中国北方干旱草原地带、黄河"几"字形弯曲环绕的内陆资源型城市，在历史上曾经是游牧文明和农耕文明交错并存的特殊文化地带。其建筑历史深受蒙、藏、汉等多元文化影响。大致而言，该地区建筑变迁从古到今可以分为五个发展阶段。

第一阶段，从"行国"到"城国"的交替变迁。从秦汉以来的大量古城堡遗址（"城国"），到南北朝、唐、宋、元、明、清朝时代流动的游牧生活形态（毡帐为主，史称"行国"），鄂尔多斯的古代建筑经历了草原游牧型毡帐集群和农耕定居型边塞城堡建筑的交融和变换。这种交混存在的形态一直延续到近代王府和早期城市聚落形态里。

第二阶段，清朝以来建筑的多元化。随着清代"盟、旗、召、府"体制的建立，游牧毡包民居和汉式王府、藏式召庙三类建筑高度共融，反映了"游牧生活—贵族政治—藏传佛教"结合的社会文化和建筑特点。现存大量的历史图文和遗留的建筑，如伊金霍洛郡王府、准格尔召等都具有多元文化的特点。各旗的王府都是吸收汉式官府的等级规制和院落形式，加以民族元素装饰而成。有的王府院落同时置有蒙古包。藏传佛教召庙则规模宏大，汉式和藏式建筑结合，各有侧重。清末实行"开放蒙荒"政策后，关内"走西口"的移民又将窑洞建筑和平民院落等民居形式带入鄂尔多斯。在盟、旗的行政中心，清末的简欧样式和民国现代砖木风格建筑出现。如在伊金霍洛旗遗存的原革委会楼、旧粮库都反映了在民国时期鄂尔多斯对国际式、现代砖石建筑样式的导入。

第三阶段，新中国成立到改革开放前。1954年营建的原伊盟行政公署办公楼是鄂尔多斯最早的多层砖混结构公共建筑。同时，蒙古民族风格样式的探索也是划时代的。尤其1956年竣工的成吉思汗陵，开启了蒙古风格现代样式的探索。建筑以蒙古穹庐毡包意象为主、辅以藏传佛教建筑色蕴和汉式建筑屋檐造型的庄重，是"现代蒙古"风格建筑的成功实例。

到改革开放前，鄂尔多斯城市建筑主体仍是低层平房和少数多层公建，建筑结构以砖木、砖混结构为主。大量的一层砖瓦平房和当年的文化馆、百货大楼、长途汽车站等公共建筑，成为这个时代的记忆。

第四阶段，20世纪80年代到21世纪初。鄂尔多斯和全国同步进入现代化和城市化初期。城市出现第一个高层建筑——鄂尔多斯羊绒集团大楼和众多的多层住宅楼房，城市从"砖瓦低层时代"向"砖混、钢混高层"时代转变。90年代初，原砖瓦厂的消失和几个大型建筑公司的产生就是这个背景下的变化。

第五阶段，"撤盟设市"后到现在的大规模建设期。这是鄂尔多斯建筑发展的"黄金十年"。2002年政府决策南迁康巴什，新区从规划到建成仅仅数年就初具规模。时间短、速度快、多元建筑形式的表达和实践全面展开！这是一个在精神状态上和城市建设上充满激情的年代。这个阶段的建筑探索主要有以下四个特征。

1. **民族符号语言形式的探索**。从蒙古包、服饰和日常用具的形式中提炼民族特色，"民族性和唯一性"这个词成为公共建筑追求的标准。鄂尔多斯大剧院（蒙古帽子）、图书馆（史书）、文化宫（云）、伊金霍洛体育馆（金马鞍）和体育场（哈达）等建筑就是这种探索的成果。

2. **行政办公为主的庄重建筑模式**。政府是城市和建筑的发展枢纽，也是经济、社会、居民的服务中心。遵循功能与形式统一的原则，政府建筑取向严整、雄伟、干净、均质的美学。代表建筑是市、区党政大楼、新闻大厦、党校和乌兰木伦湖南岸的双子楼等，共同特点是追求宏伟、庄重、大气的性格。

3. **国际性的探索和表达**。适应多元开发需求和体现个性的要求，现代"国际式风格"的高层办公建筑得以大量出现。如伊泰总部、鑫通大厦和万正广场等。同时也为国际建筑师提供了新观念建筑的试验场，如鄂尔多斯博物馆、成吉思汗博物馆、鄂尔多斯美术馆等建筑的国际性实践有着强烈的时代特征。

4. **应对本土气候、环境的建筑实践**。基于鄂尔多斯的地域特点，探索可持续、节约资源、集约发展的生态绿色建筑。其中比较有代表性的如东胜老年活动中心、响沙湾沙漠酒店、伊金霍洛规划局（旧厂房再利用）等建筑。

从数百年的历史积淀，到近十年的建设高潮，鄂尔多斯在各类建筑方面都进行了比较广泛的探索和表达，进而形成了严格的规划控制体系，呈现出比较广泛的现代都市景观。

总结当下，展望未来，鄂尔多斯建筑的黄金十年使昔日的"东胜小城"扩展成"现代大都市"。一个新兴的现代生态城市在如此短暂的时间内生成，其建筑的设计和建城的机制与西方城市完全不同。在强烈的"发展"愿望和市场投资驱动下，建筑"量"的增加和"质"的提升都创造了奇迹。在我国面临城市发展模式和理念转型的新形势下，针对鄂尔多斯城市基础和环境特点，建设的理念将要更加注重"质量和可持续"，建筑也将从"造型形式符号"的探索转向"环境对应和深层次人文空间"的探索，这是国家新型城镇化的趋势，也是鄂尔多斯发展建设的重要课题。

鄂尔多斯建筑的发展、创新和模式完善必然要继续吸收国内和国际优秀城市的经验；继续保留其多元的、丰富的建筑探索；同时更要建立新的价值观，探索属于地域性建筑的新美学、新模式。

Surrounded by Yellow River with a Ω shape, Ordos is a landlocked resource-based city located in arid steppe zone in northern China, and it was a unique cultural zone where nomadic civilization and farming civilization staggered and coexisted. Architecture history has been influenced heavily by Mongolian, Tibetan and Chinese cultures. In general, the Architectural changes in this place can be classified into five stages since ancient times.

Stage one: transition from "a country on the way" to a castled country. Lots of ancient castle sites since Qin and Han dynasty proved nomadic life in Northern and Southern Dynasties, Tang, Song, Yuan, Ming and Qing Dynasty (yurts were the main house, recorded as "country on the way"). During that time, ancient architectures of Ordos experienced integration and transformation between steppe nomadic yurt cluster and sedentary farming frontier castle. This mixed formation continued in the modern palaces and early urban patterns.

Stage two: diversified architectures since Qing Dynasty. Nomadic yurts, Chinese palaces and Tibetan temples, these three kind of architects were highly integrated thanks to the implement of "League, Banner, State, palace" system in Qing Dynasty. This inflected the architect features and social culture in the combination of nomadic life, noble politics and Tibetan Buddhism. A number of existing historic date and pictures and buildings including Ejinhoro Prince Palace, Junger temple are all with multi-cultural features. Palace in every banner absorbed the level regulation and Courtyard form in Han Dynasty, ornamented with ethnic elements, while some palace even set up yurts. Buddha temples are in large scales, while combined with Chinese and Tibetan architectures, they shares different key points. After the policy of "opening up Mongolian wasteland" in late Qing Dynasty, migration in the inner land brought Ordos more living building forms, such as cave dwelling construction and civilian courtyard. In the administrative centers of leagues and banners traces of European style in Qing Dynasty and modern timber architectures can be found, take former Revolutionary Committee building and old grain depot in Ejinhoro Banner as examples, they all showed that Ordos imported international and modern timber architectures in the period of the republic of china.

Stage three: After the liberation to before the reform and opening up. Former administrative office building Ikechosau League built in 1954 was the earliest multi-level public building in brick-concrete structure. Exploration of Mongolia nationality was epoch-making at that time. Particularly, the Mausoleum of Genghis Khan completed in 1956 opened exploration of modern style in Mongolia. Buildings are themed as Mongolia yurts, and decorated with Tibetan Buddhist architectural colors and the solemnity of buildings in Han dynasty, these are the succeed architectures in modern Mongolian style. Before reform and opening up, the main bodies of the building in Ordos were still low-level flat and few multi-level public building with a structure of brick and brick-concrete. A number of one-story dwellings built of brick and tile and public buildings like museums, stores and Inter-city bus stations; these are the memories of that era.

Stage four: 1980s to early 21st century. Ordos stepped into the early stage of modernization and urbanization together with this whole country. The first high-level building in this city--Erdos Cashmere Group Building together with plenty of multi-level residential buildings witnessed the transition of this city from "brick and low layer era" to "brick, steel and concrete high-rise era". It was under this background that brick and tile factory disappeared while several large architecture companies came into eyes in the early 1990s.

Stage five: after "changing league into city" to large-scale construction period. This was a golden decade for architectural development in Ordos. Government decided to move Kangbashi toward south, and the construction of new district has already been scaled just in a few years. As a result, planning and practicing of multiple architectural forms with a high speed in a limited time begin to roll. This is an enthusiastic era for both spiritual and architectural. Architecture exploration in this stage mainly has four features as followed.

  1. Exploration into the language forms of nationalist symbols. Refining nationalist features out of yurts, clothing and daily utensils, nationality and uniqueness became standard of Public buildings. Ordos Theater (looks like a Mongolian hat), library (historic book), cultural palace (clouds), Ejinhoro Sports Stadium (golden saddle) and sports stadium (Hada) are all the achievements of this kind of exploration.

  2. Architecture model of solemn administrative office. Government is the core axis in the development of city and architecture, as well as a center of economic, social and residential services. According to the principle of unifying functions and formations, governing architectures stress on neat, clean, majestic, homogeneous aesthetics. Representative buildings including Municipal and District Administration Buildings, News Building, Twin Buildings on the south bank of Ulanmulun River, common feature of these buildings are the character of being majestic, solemn and gorgeous.

  3. International exploration and expression. Thanks to the multiple development demands and personality requirements, modern high-level office buildings in "international Style" are able to emerge in large quantity, such as headquarter of Yitai, Xin Tong Building and Wanzheng Square, etc. meanwhile, these provide a testing ground to international architects to building new type of buildings. International practices on buildings like Ordos Museum, Genghis Khan Museum, and Ordos Art Gallery and so on have strong characteristics of times.

  4. Construction practice to the local climate, environment. Based on the regional characteristics, Ordos tries to explore ecologic buildings with sustainable, resource conserving, and intensive developing features, among which we can see the representative buildings like Dongsheng Entertainment Center for Aged People, Xiangshawan Desert Hotel, Ejinhoro Planning Bureau and some others.

  From the historic accumulation for centuries to the climax in recent ten years, Ordos has explored widely in every architectural field, which resulted in a strict planning controlling system, and thus Ordos has a really diversified modern urban landscape.

  Ordos has successfully changed Dongsheng town into modern large city in golden ten years by summarizing currency and prospecting future. That is the fine reason for why a new-born modern ecologic city has been built in such a limited time, and with a totally different design and mechanism on building with western countries. Drove by market investment and strong desire to develop, quality and quantity of building are all promoted amazingly. Under a condition that our country is now facing the transformation on the City development mode and concept, architectural concept would stress more on quality and sustainable according to the urban base and environmental features of Ordos. Meanwhile, exploration of architectures would turn to environmentally and deep-seated cultural space instead of forms of symbols; this is not only a new trend of national urbanization, but also important subject of the development and construction in Ordos.

  Development, innovation and mode of architecture in Ordos definitely need to learn from the superlatives in and out of China, maintaining the exploration on diverse and colorful architectures. At the same time, Ordos should set up new sense of worth, to search for new mode and aesthetics of regional architectures.

一、历史建筑

苏里格庙
Sulige Temple

位于鄂托克旗，占地面积 1000 亩，建筑面积 43200 平方米，相传最初建于 1228 年，开启藏传佛教在鄂尔多斯地区早期传播，1907 年修建了现今所见的苏里格庙。

局部 Section

全景 Panorama

苏里格庙会 Sulige temple fair

准格尔召
Jungar Temple

位于准格尔旗准格尔召镇，建于明代，历经清代、民国历次扩建。木刻、砖雕、绘画、壁毯做工考究，细致逼真，栩栩如生。整个建筑气象宏伟，雕梁画栋，飞檐斗栱，金琉碧瓦。建筑布局严谨、风格迥异的堂殿鳞比，疏密有致。

全景 Panorama

白塔 White tower

大独宫 Single House

菩提济度寺
Bodhi Jidu Temple

位于杭锦旗，建于明朝，重修于 2006 年，建筑形式和装饰手法，体现了汉藏两种庙宇建筑风格，形象生动，别具一格。

佛事活动 Buddhist activity

全景 Panorama

乌审召
Uxin Temple

位于乌审旗乌审召镇，占地面积达 40000 多平方米，建筑面积达 4300 多平方米。庙内的佛塔结构造型独特，召内设有三所佛学机构。鄂尔多斯佛教协会设在此。

全景 Panorama

局部 Section

细部 Details

Architectural Features | 247

成吉思汗陵
Genghis Khan Mausoleum

　　成吉思汗陵，始建于1954年，建筑风格融合了汉、藏、蒙多种元素。它以优美的草原环境，神秘的人文景观显示着草原帝王陵的雄姿，是全国重点文物保护单位，中国旅游胜地四十佳，全国文化产业示范基地、国家国防教育示范基地、国家5A级旅游景区。成吉思汗祭祀被国务院列入首批国家级非物质文化遗产名录。

全景 Panorama

局部 Section

内景 Interior

Architectural Features | 249

郡王府
Jun Wangfu Palace

位于伊金霍洛旗阿镇，为内蒙古自治区重点文物保护单位，筹建于1928年，落成于1936年，总占地面积2200平方米，属砖、木、石结构，具有浓郁的民族特色和地方特色。据《伊克昭盟志》记载，郡王府"画阁雕梁、龙文凤彩、备极富丽。"

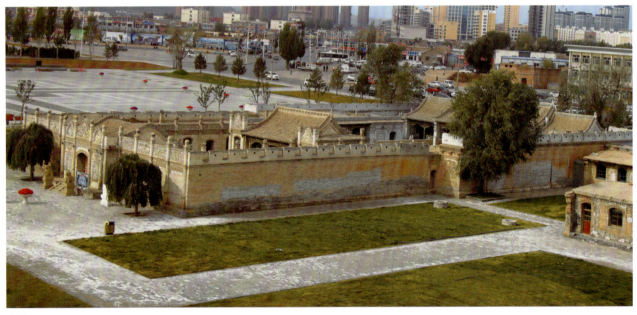

全景 Panorama

宅门 Housedoor

前院正房 Main House in Front Yard

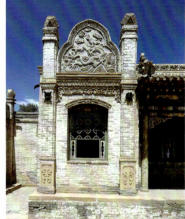
局部 Section

后院正房 Main House in Back Yard

细部 Detail

王府内部 Interior of Palace

王府内部 Interior of Palace

Architectural Features | 251

伊克昭盟党政办公楼
Ikechosau League Party and government office

  位于东胜区,始建于1954年,建筑面积4070平方米,后增建盟委办公楼。共同特点是简约、庄重,力求体现地域性。

原盟行政公署办公楼 Former Administrative office

原盟党委办公楼 Former Party Committee Office

二、"盟改市"后的建筑
Buildings after "League to City"

鄂尔多斯青铜文化博物馆
Ordos Bronze Culture Museum

位于东胜铁西区,总占地面积约为4.63公顷,建筑面积约3万平方米,总建筑高度达到58.1米。整体设计从出土青铜器"匈奴王冠"中获得灵感,以现代建筑手法重新解构,塑造了独特的具有雕塑感的王者之冠主题建筑形象。

全景 Panorama

侧面 Profile

主入口 Main entrance

鄂尔多斯恰特
Ordos Theater

位于东胜旧区，总建筑面积0.88万平方米，原建于20世纪70年代，21世纪初改造装修，采用了当地生态、民族、历史等地域元素。例如暗红色取自于众多藏传佛寺；装饰图案取材于蒙古头饰；动物造型取材于草原青铜文化。

改造前 Before reconstruction　　　　　　　　　　　　细部 Detail

入口大厅 Entrance Hall　　　　　　　　　　　　内景 Interior

局部 Section

正面 Frontage

科技会展中心
Science and Technology Exhibition Center

位于东胜老城区，建筑面积约为 2.34 万平方米，共 9 层，是集科技馆、青少年宫、图书馆、文化馆为一体的综合楼。

全景 Panorama

行星展厅 Planetary hall

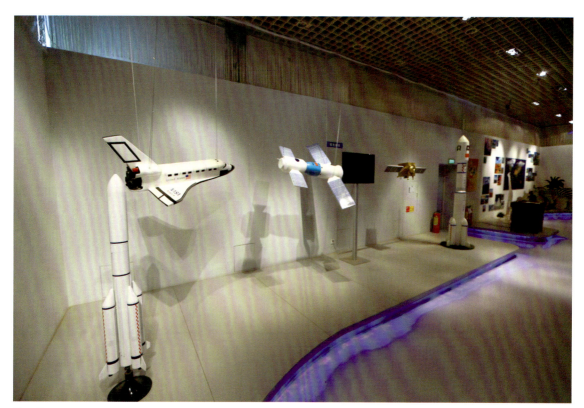

航天展厅 The space hall

物理实验室 Physics Lab

Architectural Features

总平面图 General plans

立面图 Elevation

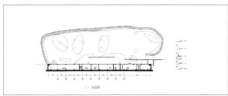

剖面图 Section drawing

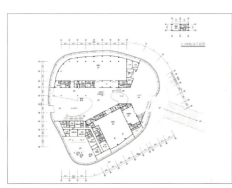

一层平面图 First floor plan

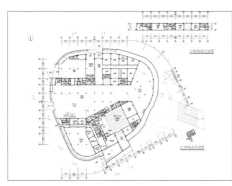

二层平面图 Second floor plan

全景 Panorama

鄂尔多斯博物馆
Ordos Museum

位于康巴什新区，于2006年建设。占地面积为2.78公顷，建筑面积为4.12万平方米，是地下一层，地上四层，局部八层的综合性博物馆。配套有专业展厅、大型学术报告厅、办公室、会议室、贵宾接待室，同时，还配备有餐厅、地下停车场等多个辅助设施。

设计理念为一块坚固的巨型石头象征着永恒，古铜色的金属外表面记录着鄂尔多斯悠久的历史文化，硕大饱满形体蕴含的力度展现着鄂尔多斯面向未来的创新精神。

鄂尔多斯博物馆
Ordos Museum

入口处 Entrance

细部 Detail

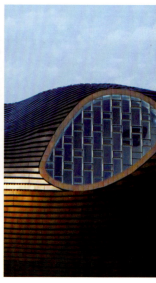

细部 Detail

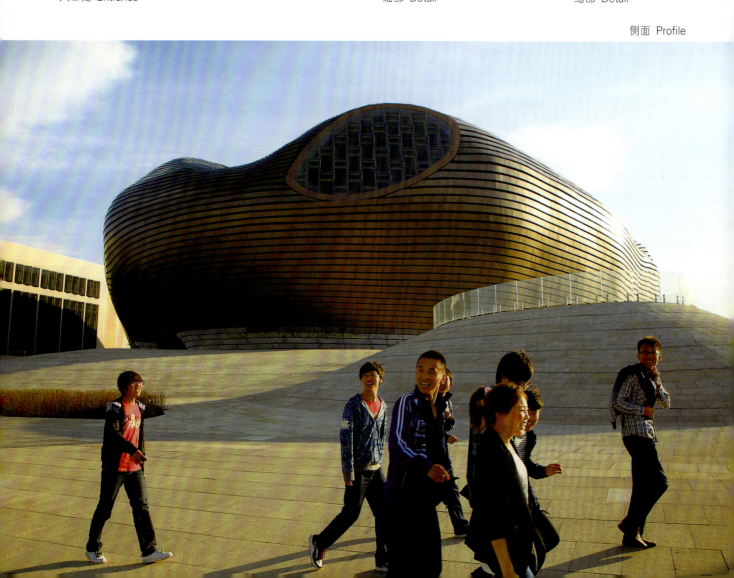

侧面 Profile

内景细部 Interior detail　　内景局部 Interior section

正面 Frontage

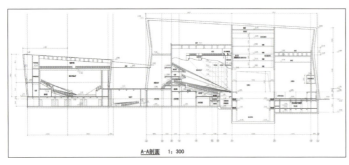

A-A 剖面图 A-A cross-sectional view

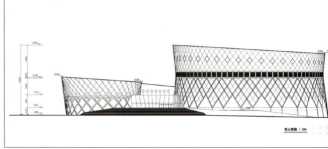

南立面图 South elevation

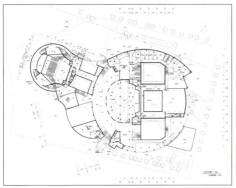

总平面图 General Plan

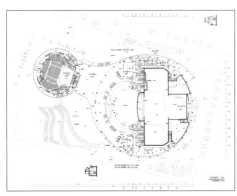

一层平面图 First floor plan

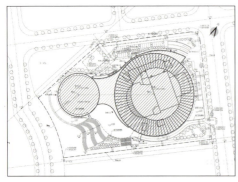

二层平面图 Second floor plan

全景 Panorama

鄂尔多斯大剧院
Ordos Grand Theater

位于康巴什新区，于2006年建设，占地面积2.27公顷，总建筑面积4.27万平方米，地下一层，地上五层。功能包括综合剧场、音乐厅、数字电影厅，以及娱乐等附属服务设施。

鄂尔多斯大剧院设计理念来源于鄂尔多斯蒙古族头饰，其中大圆为建筑主体，模拟鄂尔多斯妇女头戴，小圆模拟蒙古族男士帽子，由男士帽子的飘带与大圆连接形成共享大厅，整体设计新颖，是现代与民族风格的有机统一。

鄂尔多斯大剧院
Ordos Grande Theater

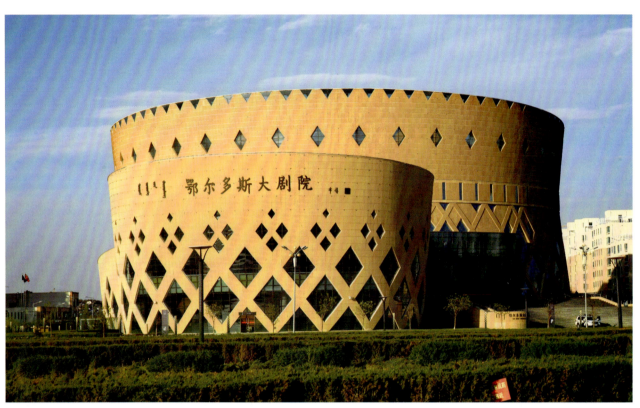

正面 Frontage

夜景 Night View

主入口 Main Entrance

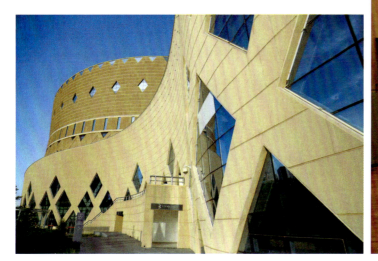

局部 Section

音乐厅 Music Hall

内景细部 Interior Detail

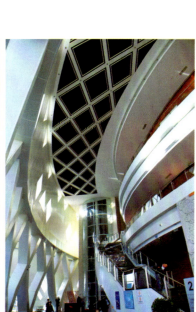

内景细部 Interior Detail

鄂尔多斯文化艺术中心
Ordos Culture and Art Centre

位于康巴什新区，于 2006 年建设。占地面积 2.25 公顷，总建筑面积 4.23 万平方米，是地下一层、地上六层集文化活动、娱乐休闲及群艺馆办公于一体的大型综合性建筑。

设计理念为"天圆地方"，建筑上部乳白色的轻盈变形体象征着天空、白云、空气、水和乳汁，隐喻着女性、舞蹈、飘逸的哈达与自由、浪漫、吉祥；下部浮动的方形象征着草原和大地，隐喻着男性、力量、阳刚之气和朴实方正的含义，方与圆的结合体现了人与自然的对话和宇宙模型的对应。

全景 Panorama

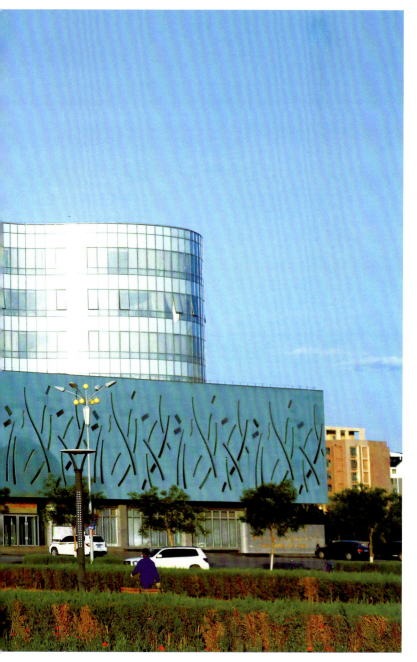

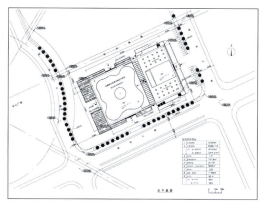

总平面图 General Plan

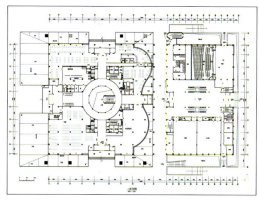

一层平面图 First floor plan

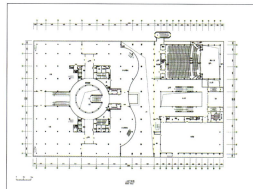

二层平面图 Second floor plan

1-1 剖面图 1-1 Elevation

鄂尔多斯文化艺术中心
Ordos Culture and Art Centre

夜景 Night view

侧面 Profile

细部 Detail

民族展厅 Nationality Exhibition Hall

内景细部 Interior Detail

工艺品展厅 Arts and Crafts Exhibition hall

健身房 Gym

局部 Section

放映厅 Video hall

鄂尔多斯图书馆
Ordos Library

位于康巴什新区，于 2006 年建设，占地面积 2.12 公顷，总建筑面积 4.17 万平方米，地下一层，地上八层，包括五大功能区。设计理念为借意《蒙古源流》、《蒙古秘史》、《蒙古黄金史》三本蒙古历史巨著。

全景 Panorama

背面 Back Facade

二楼休息厅 Lounge on second floor

书店 Bookstore

鄂尔多斯国际会展中心
Ordos International Exhibition Center

位于康巴什新区，于 2007 年建设。总占地面积 8.34 公顷，总建筑面积 4.75 万平方米，由会议中心和展厅两部分组成，其造型设计中融入了多种体现蒙元文化的符号和元素。入口会堂为蒙古包造型，3 个大展厅是马鞍造型。

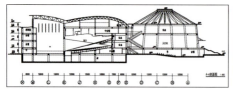

A-A 剖面图　A-A cross-sectional view

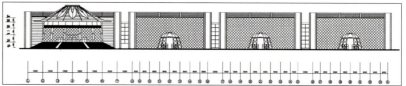

南立面　South elevation

全景　Panorama

总平面图 General plan

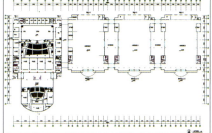
一层平面图 First floor plan

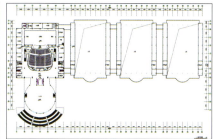
二层平面图 Second floor plan

鸟瞰 Aerial View

鄂尔多斯国际会展中心
Ordos International Exhibition Center

夜景 Night view

局部 Section

多功能厅 Multifunctional Hall

侧入口 Side entrance

休息大厅一角 A corner of lounge

入口处 Entrance

入口大厅 Entrance Hall

Architectural Features | 275

东胜全民健身中心
Dongsheng People's Fitness Center

位于东胜铁西区，总占地面积约49.3公顷，总建筑面积15.05万平方米。由体育场、综合体育馆、水上运动中心、体育商业中心组成。体育场活动屋盖采用钢缆绳牵引方式驱动。

设计以"灵动飘逸"为主题，结构拱券造型设计取自蒙古民族传统工具"弓"的造型，屋顶上钢结构主拱券高达129米，跨度320米，犹如一张巨大的弯弓，直立天际；拱券上的钢拉索又似传统民族乐器一根根琴弦。

全景 Panorama

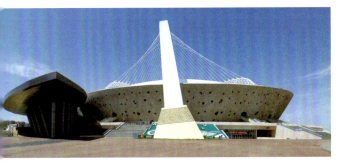
侧面 Profile

乒乓球馆 Table tennis stadium

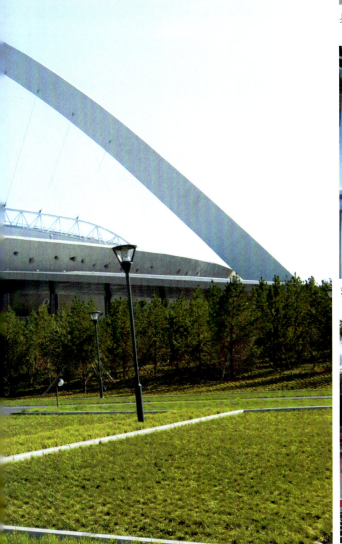

羽毛球馆 Badminton stadium

运动场内景 Playground interior

Architectural Features | 277

全景 Panorama

伊金霍洛旗影剧院
Ejinhoro Banner cinema

位于伊金霍洛旗阿镇，于 2009 年建设，占地面积 6.81 公顷，总建筑面积 3.63 万平方米，由剧院，音乐厅，多功能厅组成。整体立意为"前行金帐"。建筑造型创意来源于成吉思汗移动的宫殿，在运行中迸发出强劲的韵律和节奏。

夜景 Night view

鸟瞰 Aerial View

细部 Section

内景 Interior

Architectural Features

伊金霍洛旗体育活动中心
Ejinhoro Banner Sports Center

　　位于伊金霍洛旗阿镇，于 2009 年建设。总占地面积占地 6.7 公顷，总建筑面积 3.86 万平方米，总高为 23.98 米，结构形式为大跨度空间钢结构。本工程是集比赛馆、游泳馆、训练馆及公众休闲娱乐功能为一体的中型综合体育馆。

夜景 Night View　　　　　　　　　　　　　　　正面 Frontage

乒乓球馆 Table tennis stadium

游泳馆 Natatorium

主入口 Main entrance

内景细部 Interior detail

体操馆 Gymnastic hall

夜景 Night view　　　　　　　　　　　　　　　　　　　　　　　　　细部 Detail

鄂尔多斯市机场
Ordos Airport

位于伊金霍洛镇，于 2009 年开工建设，建筑面积为 11.913 万平方米，主体共分为三层，可满足年旅客吞吐量 1000 万人次运营需求，航站楼设计理念为"草原雄鹰"，中央建筑为巨型现代蒙古包造型，整体建筑造型新颖、独特、现代，同时又蕴含有丰富的蒙古民族文化元素。

全景 Panorama

内景 Interior

康巴什新区第一幼儿园
1st Kindergarten of Kangbashi New Area

位于康巴什新区，2011年开工建设，净用地面积1公顷，建筑面积0.47万平方米，建筑造型为孩子的小脚丫，寓意活泼、天真、可爱。

全景 Panorama

局部 Section

幼儿园门口 Front door

活动室 Playroom

休息室 Llounge

细部 Detail

室外活动 Outdoor activity

鄂尔多斯市委党校
Ordos Party School

位于康巴什新区，占地面积 200 多亩，总建筑面积 6.5 万平方米，是集教学、科研、办公、餐饮、公寓、健身于一体的现代化新校区。校园环境优雅整洁，教学设施配套齐全。

综合楼全景 Panorama of complex building

综合楼正面 Frontage of complex building

综合楼细部 Detail of complex building

综合楼侧面 Profile of complex building

综合楼背面 Backside of complex building

综合楼大厅 Complex building Hall

Architectural Features | 287

鄂尔多斯市党政大楼
Ordos Party and government office

位于康巴什新区，于 2004 年建设。现代的建筑风格与简洁质朴的建筑形象，突出了党政大楼宏伟、庄重的特点。

夜景 Night view

全景 Panorama

细部 Detail

入口 Entrance

连廊 Corridor

侧面 Profile

入口大厅 Entrance Hall

国泰大厦
Cathay Building

位于乌兰木伦河核心高层区，占地面积为 17.55 公顷，总建筑面积为 70.17 万平方米，建 6 座百米高楼，其中 2 座为 22 层，高度 100 米；2 座 26 层，高度 120 米和 2 座为 42 层，高度 184 米。该项目是鄂尔多斯市标志性建筑。

背面 Back Facade

正面临乌兰木伦河南岸绿带 Section Greenbelt on the South of UlanMulun River

局部 Section

细部 Detail

东胜区党政大楼
Dongsheng Party and government office

　　位于东胜铁西区,共8层,整体坐北面南,是东胜城区的标志建筑之一。建筑整体追求简洁、质朴,体量厚重,建筑的形式与功能相得益彰。

正面 Section

局部 Section

主入口 Main entrance

大厅 Hall

Architectural Features

侧面 Profile

全景 Panorama

鄂尔多斯国土大厦
Ordos Territory Hall

位于康巴什新区,于2005年开工建设。占地面积1.42公顷,建筑面积8.9万平方米。本工程采用了"等边三角形"的设计元素,曲直结合的线条力图表现政府建筑的庄重和地域特色相结合。

全景 Panorama

鄂尔多斯新闻大厦
Ordos News Building

位于康巴什新区,于 2006 年开工建设,占地面积 1.65 公顷,建筑面积 4.42 万平方米。建筑符号取材于眼球、镜头的圆形,表达"看世界"的主题。

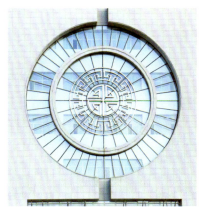

细部 Detail

正面 Section

恒信大酒店
Hengxin Hotel

泰华锦江国际大酒店
Taihua jinjiang International Hotel

鄂尔多斯皇冠假日酒店
Ordos Crowne Plaza

位于东胜区，是鄂尔多斯市最早兴建的一家五星级酒店，总占地面积28.8公顷，建筑面积7.1万平方米。建筑风格和色彩与当地自然生态环境融为一体。

局部 Section

全景 Panorama

会议室 Conference room

游泳池 Swimming pool

总统套房 Presidential suite

多功能厅 Multifunctional hall

Architectural Features | 299

建一公馆
Jianyi Mansion

全景 Panorama

公馆入口 Mansion entrance

入口大厅 Entrance hall

乌兰国际大酒店
Ulan International Hotel

博源豪生大酒店
Boyuan HoJo Grand Hotel

全景 Panorama

健身房 Gym

游泳馆 Swimming pool

餐厅 Festaurant

客房 Guest room

万佳会所
Manka club

全景 Panorama

主楼正面 Frontage of main building

主楼入口 Entrance of main building

达拉特旗体育中心
Dalad Sports Center

位于树林召镇，于 2009 年建设，总占地为 4.18 公顷，建筑面积为 2.13 万平方米，是集文化、艺术、体育竞赛于一体的大型现代化全民健身公益体育设施。设计理念借用了蒙古包、马鞍等元素。

背景 Back facade　　　　　入口处 Entrance

正面 Panorama

羽毛球馆 Badminton stadium

篮球馆 Basketball stadium

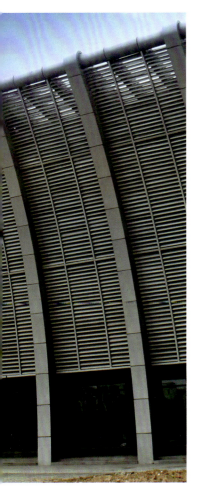

细部 Detail

Architectural Features | 305

矿物厅 Mineral hall

恐龙厅 Dinosaur hall

鄂托克旗地质博物馆

位于乌兰镇，于2009年开工建设，总占地面积为3.57公顷，总建筑面积为1.37万平方米。馆内设有恐龙厅、地球厅、矿物厅和民俗厅等7个展厅，记录了鄂托克旗地质演化史以及自然环境变迁的重要信息。

设计理念取义于本旗西部桌子山造型，门厅取自恐龙腿的元素。

全景 Panorama

内景细部 Interior detail

总平面图 General plan　　背面 Back facade　　主入口 Main entrance

鄂托克旗老年活动中心
Otog banner Entertainment Center for Aged People

位于乌兰镇，2009年开工建设，总占地面积为1.30公顷，总建筑面积为0.84万平方米。整体造型以两个椭圆形体交错组合，体现了内在的力度和气势。

背面 Back facade

鸟瞰 Aerial view

正面 Frontage

准格尔旗南山社区
Jungar Banner Nanshan community

位于薛家湾镇，依山而建，建筑以灯塔造型，将功能、形式、特色装饰和生态环境融合为一。

细部 Detail

服务大厅 Service hall

全景 Panorama

局部 Section

全景 Panorama

鄂托克前旗涛龙宫
Taolong Palace of Otog front banner

　　位于敖勒召其镇，本工程原为旗影剧院，后结合影剧院两侧商业建筑改造形成目前的涛龙宫，浑然一体，主体建筑民族特色与现代感相结合，总占地面积为0.51公顷，总建筑面积0.54万平方米，是举办会议、歌舞表演、大型文艺晚会的综合场所。

局部 Section

入口大厅 Entrance hall

表演厅 Performing hall

鄂托克前旗草原大舞台
Otog front banner prairie Stage

位于上海庙镇，于 2010 年开工建设，是一座集演出、餐饮为一体的联欢性质的演艺建筑，建筑面积 1.2 万平方米，建筑平面是一个直径为 99.9 米的圆形。设计灵感来自于蒙古传统聚落建筑，总体高度为 45.9 米，24 个直径为 3.9 米的镶嵌着金色云纹的红色石柱围绕建筑主体排列。

全景 Panorama

主入口 Main entrance

入口细部 Entrance detail

细部 Detail

第六章 雕塑与装饰

Chapter Six

Sculptures
& Decoration

鄂尔多斯的雕塑及相关类型的造型艺术源远流长。不同时期的雕塑类艺术积淀了那个时代深厚的历史印迹：新石器时代的岩画记录了古人类在草原上狩猎、祭祀的情景；陶器和青铜器时代的大量遗存是人类活动在鄂尔多斯持续增强的写照，特别是众多以动物雕像为主的艺术品反映了草原游牧文明的繁荣，其中匈奴鹰形金冠是驰骋欧亚草原的匈奴帝国唯一存世的帝王专属用品；元代遗留下来的阿尔寨石窟则是一座由石雕、塑像、壁画组成的古代艺术殿堂。丰富的历史遗存为鄂尔多斯当代异彩纷呈的雕塑设计提供了本土源泉。

在快速城市化的今天，雕塑已经成为鄂尔多斯环境艺术和城市文化的组成部分。遍布于公园、广场、街区的各类雕塑，是这座新兴现代城市的独特景观。这些雕塑造型各异，工艺精致，形态优美，风格与手法鲜明，诠释着积极向上的精神面貌和深厚的文化底蕴，展现了城市的地域特色。

鄂尔多斯的雕塑具有数量大、门类多、题材广泛、特色浓厚、富有创新精神的特点。在体裁方面，宣示性雕塑以"金三角"为代表，以一个屹立在东胜区北出口的巨型金色三角体加以民族图案的装饰，寓意民族地区正处在稳定崛起的黄金时代。纪念性雕塑应首推依据成吉思汗历史题材创作的众多作品，如成吉思汗母亲雕塑和成吉思汗生平组雕等，与成吉思汗近几百年一直在鄂尔多斯草原祭祀的史实相吻合。亚洲雕塑艺术公园以23尊亚洲各国的代表性雕塑和鄂尔多斯36尊青铜器文物雕塑为第十一届亚洲艺术节在鄂尔多斯举办留下了永恒的纪念。园林景观雕塑星罗棋布于各个城镇和所有绿地公园，是人文环境和生态环境共融的象征。在形态方面，除单体独立的雕塑外，许多作品是以组合的形式出现在主题文化广场，如蒙古象棋广场、婚庆文化园、草原情公园以及综合性园林广场，具有画龙点睛的文化意义。

鄂尔多斯的城市景观壁画多以民族文化和当代发展为主题，其中乌兰木伦河两岸的大型叙事型壁画蔚为壮观，工艺精美，人物栩栩如生。

建筑装饰采用民族元素的成功典型广泛存在。比较常见的是将蒙古包的造型及构成元素抽象化，运用于穹顶线条和内部装饰。考古发现、历史记载、草原风情、生态自然等地域元素也是建筑内外装饰素材的重要来源。

Sculptures and related arts in Ordos have a long story. Sculpture article in different time were caved with deep historic signs in that time: Petro glyphs in Neolithic pictured scenes that ancient human hunting, worshiping on the grassland; lots of site in Bronze and Pottery Age showed human were growing in Ordos, especially the articles and statues based on animals reflected the prosperity, among which, the Eagle Golden Crown is the only existing exclusive product for King of The Hun Empire; A'erzhai grotto of Yuan Dynasty is an ancient art paradise consisted by statue, mural and carving. These rich historical heritages provide the source of contemporary colorful sculpture design of Ordos.

Nowadays, urbanization is really rapid, while sculpture has been an integral part of Ordos environmental art and urban culture. Sculptures spread around squares, blocks and parks are unique views in this emerging modern city. These sculptures have various shapes, sophisticated craftwork, beautiful appearances with distinctive style and techniques, interpreting positive mental outlook and rich cultural heritage, showing geographical characteristics of the city

Sculptures in Ordos share characters of large quantities and categories with innovations and wide range of topics. In terms of genre, declaratory sculpture "Golden Triangle" standing by the north exit of Dongsheng District is a represent; it is a giant golden triangle with ethnic patterns on, which means this area is now in a golden age of development and rise. Outstanding memorial sculptures would be numerous works based on the historic theme of Genghis Khan, such as Genghis Khan's Mother and serial sculptures of life of Genghis Khan, they coincide with the history that Genghis Khan Mausoleum were holding worship activities on Ordos grassland for last centuries. Sculpture made by 23 representative sculptures from each Asian country and 36 Ordos bronze sculptures in Asian Sculpture Art Park, left a lasting memory on the Eleventh Asian Arts Festival held in Ordos. It is a symbol of the combination of human environment and ecological environment to place sculptures in each town and each park. In terms of morphology, beside several single sculptures, most of sculptures are constructed by group in the theme parks; Mongolia chess square, Wedding Culture Park, Caoyuanqing Square and Comprehensive garden squares, sculpture groups in those places have key cultural significances.

Urban mural landscape in Ordos mainly adopt national culture and current development as the theme, large narrative murals on the banks of Ulanmulun River are excellent mural landscape with exquisite workmanship and visual characters.

There are large amount of examples for ethnic elements as building decorations. Commonly, shape of yurt is abstract and used as the lines on the ceilings and interior decorations. Regional elements like archaeological discoveries, historical records, prairie style, and eco nature are also vital resources of interior and exterior ornaments.

《苏勒德》雕塑
Sculpture Sulde

位于东胜北出口，取材于成吉思汗军徽造型彰显深厚的历史文化底蕴。

底部浮雕表现草原人民的生产生活场景

苏勒德局部 Section of Sulde

细部装饰 Detailed decorations

sculptures & Decoration | 317

《金三角》雕塑
sculpture Golden Triangle

该雕塑作品象征鄂尔多斯稳定快速崛起。

《翱翔》雕塑
soaring

以出土"匈奴"王冠为蓝本进行变形创造，采用动物图案纹样为装饰，具有北方草原民族历史文化特征。

sculptures & Decoration

成吉思汗史诗组雕
serial sculptures of Genghis Khan epic

五组雕塑位于康巴什新区广场，全部依据成吉思汗历史素材创作而成。

草原母亲——成吉思汗母亲以五支箭教子团结的故事
Prairie Mother, Genghis Khan's mother taught him about unity by five Arrows

海纳百川——成吉思汗知人善任，聚集人才的真实故事
Tolerant to diversity, a real story about Genghis Khan who appreciates talents and recognizes abilities

闻名世界——成吉思汗民族统一的功绩和自强不息的精神
World-famous, an expression on Self-improvement and national unity achievements of Genghis Khan

天驹行空——取材于成吉思汗的双骏战马
Galloping horses, Based on the two horses of Genghis Khan

一代天骄——表现成吉思汗的生平
The great man, a life story of Genghis Khan

sculptures & Decoration | 323

诃额伦雕塑
sculptures of Heelun

诃额伦，一代天骄成吉思汗的母亲。雕塑位于伊金霍洛旗母亲公园。

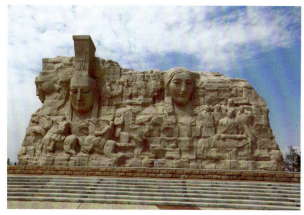
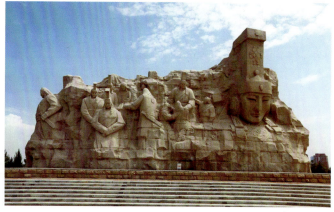

《匈奴王冠》雕塑
Huns' crown

该雕塑作品以"匈奴"王冠为蓝本,纯金冠顶镶嵌着绿松石雄鹰。造型简洁又气势不凡。

《奶茶飘香》雕塑
Fragrant Milky Tea

该雕塑以奶茶飘香水景为主体，营造热烈而又祥和的草原气息。

鄂尔多斯时代广场主雕
main sculptures of Ordos Times Square

该雕塑作品位于东胜区时代广场,寓意鄂尔多斯市的八个旗市和四大支柱产业。

《天·元》雕塑
Sculpture of sky and Ground

《天元》造型集宏大与单纯、民族性与现代性于一体,寓意可持续循环发展的伊金霍洛。

亚洲雕塑艺术园作品
works in Asian Sculpture Park

高山流水——寓意音乐的出神入化
Lofty mountains & flowing water, Meaning superb music

异域的月光——马尔代夫的作品
Exotic moonlight, work of Maldives

生态循环——解释生命的变化与轮回
Eco-Cycle, symbolize life changing and rebirthing

工业缪斯
Industrial Muse

看世界——双面不同民族童像，象征亚洲人民和平相处
Witness, Different ethnic children on two sides symbolizing Asians living in peace

不丹印象
Impression of Bhutan

少女与象——寓意人与自然和谐相处
Maiden and Elephant, Harmony between man and nature

似水年华——缅甸作品
Lost Years, work of Burma

草原人民生活雕塑
sculptures of Mongolian people's life

前三幅为奶食制作过程 Process of making mike food

童趣 Playing children

鄂尔多斯婚礼雕塑
Ordos Wedding sculpture

分辫出嫁 Braiding before wedding

惜别父母 Farewell to parents

祝福 Blessing

喜迎宾客 Greeting guests

sculptures & Decoration | 335

运动题材雕塑
sculpture on sport theme

sculptures & Decoration | 337

记忆中的家园
home in memory

街头雕塑
Street sculpture

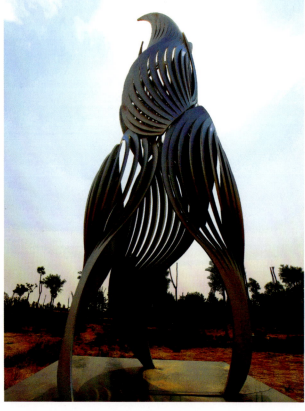

sculptures & Decoration | 341

街头雕塑
Street sculpture

街头雕塑
Street sculpture

sculptures & Decoration | 345

浮雕景墙
Relief wall

浮雕景墙弧长 30 米、高 8 米，并利用植物塑造高低错落的色带，营造入口的礼仪感。

sculptures & Decoration | 347

郡王府砖石浮雕（民国时期）
Brick reliefs of Prince's Mansion

sculptures & Decoration

白马雕塑
sculptures of white horses

20世纪80年代初,伊金霍洛旗阿勒腾席热镇三年蝉联内蒙古自治区爱国卫生"阿吉奈"银马奖,被自治区命名为全区第一个"文明镇"、被国家命名为全国"卫生镇",特设此雕塑以示纪念。

鄂托克旗《圣火》雕塑
Flame, Otog banner

雕塑造型取材蒙古包的"灶火"——火撑的造型,雕塑主体中部由柱子构成,体现"火"的至阳本质,柱子下部是火苗的造型,柱子上部是金色的《圣火》蒙文诗。

鄂托克旗《神鹰的传说》雕塑
Legend of the Condor, Otog banner

采用铸铜做旧仿青铜器工艺,展翅欲飞的神鹰透雕表现关于神鹰的当地民间传说。

乌审旗独贵龙广场群雕
sculpture blocks of Uxin Banner Duguilong Square

该雕塑作品反映席尼喇嘛带领自己的安达反抗王公贵族统治压迫的情景。

乌审旗《大牛角造型门》雕塑
Horn shaped gateway, Uxin banner

达拉特旗《马头琴及哈达》雕塑
Mongol Stringed Instrument& Hada, Dalad Banner

三色哈达连接成巨型拱门,并用马头琴造型和浮雕表达出内蒙古人民的热情好客。

达拉特旗《龙虎》雕塑
Dragon and tiger, Dalad Banner

《鄂尔多斯史诗》景观效果 Landscape of Ordos epic

乌兰木伦河壁画之鄂尔多斯史诗
Ordos epic, Mural on the Bank of Ulanmulun River

局部 Section

鄂尔多斯史诗壁画反映了远古时期、青铜文化、历史变迁、成吉思汗祭祀文化、三大蒙古历史巨著、草原风情及近代红色故事等主题内容。

局部 Section

乌兰木伦河壁画之一代天骄群英谱
Collection of the Great Men, Mural on the Bank of Ulanmulun River

成吉思汗在其不平凡的一生中,四方英杰聚集于"一代天骄帐下,创造人类史上空前伟大的奇迹"。

局部 Section

《一代天骄群英谱》景观效果 Landscape of Collection of the Great Men

局部 Section

sculptures & Decoration | 357

局部 Section

乌兰木伦河壁画之高原上的京都统万城
Tongwan City—capital on prairie, River murals

《高原上的京都一统万城》景观效果 Landscape of Tongwan City—capital on prairie

整个画面描绘匈奴贵族赫连勃勃在鄂尔多斯高原建立大夏国,中心画面是各方诸侯在统万城"觐见国王赫连勃勃"的场景,两侧分别是"沙城牧羊"和"塞外商旅"的内容。

景观效果 Landscape

乌兰木伦河壁画之历史巨著蒙古源流
Erdeniin Tobchi, one of the three historic masterpieces

局部 Section

以《蒙古源流》的历史内容为蓝本绘制。蒙古的崛起及成吉思汗史诗,至清初蒙古的历史文化及佛教传播,历述元明两代蒙古各汗的事迹及蒙古民间传说、诗歌。《蒙古源流》与《元秘史》、《蒙古黄金史》合称为蒙古民族的三大历史著作。

局部 Section

《鄂尔多斯婚礼》景观效果 Landscape of Ordos wedding

乌兰木伦河壁画之鄂尔多斯婚礼
Ordos wedding, Mural on the Bank of Ulanmulun River

局部 Section

鄂尔多斯婚礼，程序繁密，礼节讲究，格调高雅。其场面宏大，喜庆气氛热烈而浓郁；其情节亦庄亦谐，充满了生活情趣；其祝词深沉、凝炼，饱含了人生的哲理；其服饰既绚烂华贵，又不失端庄典雅。洋洋洒洒三天三夜的过程，歌河长流，舞姿奔放，豪饮通宵达旦⋯⋯

2006年，鄂尔多斯婚礼已被列入国家首批非物质文化遗产名录。

局部 Section

石窟片段 Grotto Fragment

乌兰木伦河石窟
Ulanmulun River Grotto

根据鄂尔多斯市境内的石窟遗址进行复制、创作。

石窟局部 Grotto section

石窟局部 Grotto section

sculptures & Decoration

石窟片段 Grotto Fragment

石窟局部 Grotto section

石窟局部 Grotto section

sculptures & Decoration

石窟局部 Grotto section

石窟局部 Grotto section

鄂托克旗阿尔寨石窟
A-er zhai Grotto in Otog Banner

为元代遗址，保留有精美壁画。

顶棚装饰
Ceiling decoration

现代公共建筑仿蒙古包"穹庐"顶造型，经过设计加工，将使用功能与审美功能巧妙地结合起来，造成一种豪放而又优柔的气氛。

sculptures & Decoration

鄂尔多斯飞机场装饰
decoration of Ordos Airport

取材于草原牧民生活场景、成吉思汗史诗、祖国大家庭五十六个民族等，表达各民族和谐、奋进的精神。

室外装饰
Exterior decoration

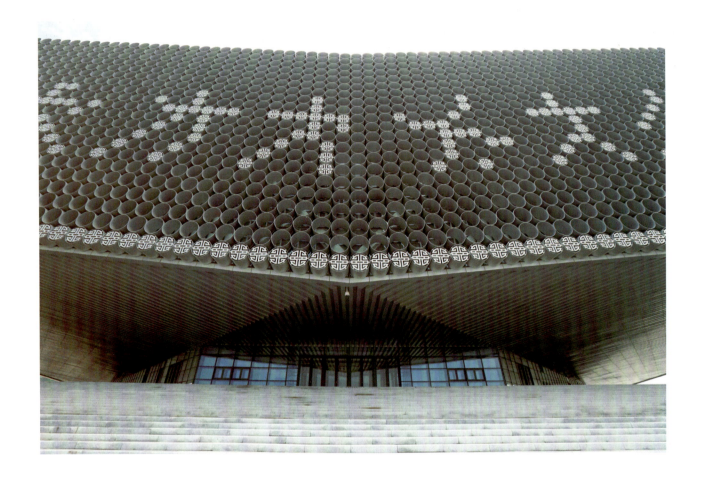

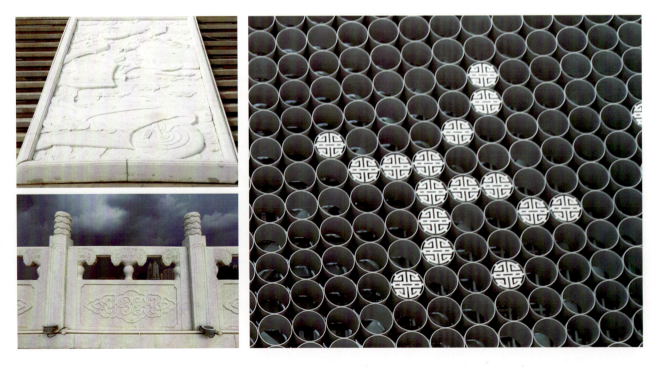